INFERNO
in the Lost Pines

© 2013 by TGS International, a wholly owned subsidiary of Christian Aid Ministries, Berlin, Ohio.

All rights reserved. No part of this book may be used, reproduced, or stored in any retrieval system, in any form or by any means, electronic or mechanical, without written permission from the publisher except for brief quotations embodied in critical articles and reviews.

ISBN: 978-1-939084-76-7

Cover and layout design: Megan Yoder

Front cover photos: © William Laird

Printed in the USA

For more information about Christian Aid Ministries, see page 225.

TGS000721

Published by:
TGS International
P.O. Box 355
Berlin, Ohio 44610 USA
Phone: 330-893-4828
Fax: 330-893-2305
www.tgsinternational.com

INFERNO
in the Lost Pines

Katrina Hoover

TABLE OF CONTENTS

    Principal Characters 7

1. A History of Survival. 9
2. Ten Families Along Highway 21 19
3. Four Families Along Highway 71 33
4. The Hot Summer 37
5. The Strong Wind. 51
6. The Tree That Snapped 59
7. The Runaway Scrape of 2011 71
8. Escapees 75
9. Saving Lives First. 93
10. The Night No One Slept. 107
11. Day of Labor. 121
12. Banding Together 141
13. Pets in the Inferno. 147
14. Going On in Faith 153
15. Homes Along Highway 21 .163
16. Homes Along Highway 71 .181
17. Replanting and Rebuilding 187
18. Christmas and New Houses 199
19. The Town That Has Always Survived. 211

    Endnotes. 219

    About the Author 223

PRINCIPAL CHARACTERS

RESIDENTS CLOSE TO HIGHWAY 21

Dean and Debra Pahlow—lived in "the house that God built" on Alum Creek Drive

Mike and Shirley Gibbons—owners of Itsatown and windmill

Wesley and Margaret Peschke—former missionaries and owners of bottle house

Patty Timmons—crafter of sun catchers; had a pet dog, Shadow

Adam and Cindy Cruz—Christians opposed by family; lived in house with rock walls

Nicholas Cowey—worker at McKinney Roughs Nature Park and collector of books and furs

Efrain and Debi Canava—lived in two-story log cabin

Alan Donaldson—Bastrop firefighter and voracious reader

Rene and Kathy Rizk—owners of mechanic shop

Bill and Patsy Ludwig—owners of property with 370 trees

RESIDENTS CLOSE TO HIGHWAY 71

Larry Miller—farmer with high-quality goats

Jimmy Mack—world traveler and former parachuter

George Martinez—Bastrop firefighter from Tahitian Village

Ryan Terranova—gas station attendant and owner of red minivan, Betsy

OTHER CHARACTERS

Michael Fisher—emergency management coordinator for Bastrop County

Chief Henry Perry—head of the Bastrop Fire Department

Josh Gill—district fire chief

Judge McDonald—judge of Bastrop County

Gayle Wilhelm—Judge McDonald's secretary

Troy Walters—Bastrop County Animal Shelter

1

A HISTORY OF SURVIVAL

The sparks lit up the dry blades of grass and licked up the warm rosin in the pine needles. The heated rosin turned into a cloud of gas, quickly bursting into orange flame like a candle. The fire crackled, jumping from needle to needle, more rosin vaporizing and more clouds of gas igniting. The fallen electric lines sizzled and snapped.

Next, the fire heated a twig with a cluster of needles. Like a spontaneous friendship, the vaporized rosin enveloped the dry twig. The next instant, the twig burst into flames.

The flames from the twig heated a branch full of twigs. All of the rosin in that branch turned into a cloud of gas, and the whole branch combusted in a rush of orange flame. Pushed by the unrelenting wind, this larger flame rushed ahead, licking more needles, more twigs, and more branches.

Then, the flame reached a small tree. The tree was so hot and dry from the summer conditions of 2011 that in no time it was heated to 140 degrees Fahrenheit, the pivotal temperature at which rosin turns into a cloud of gas. With a *whoosh* the tree went up in flame, as fast as a candle wick.

Had it not been windy, the fire would have moved slowly from needle to twig to branch to tree, following the fuel. The firefighters would have had plenty of time to arrive on the scene and put out the fire. They had put out many wildfires before, even in the heat and drought.

But this time it was very windy.

The leap from needle to twig to branch to tree happened in seconds, and Bastrop County began to burn.

The city of Bastrop has a history of survival. Before anyone thought of the name *Bastrop,* a loblolly pine tree sprouted there. It survived, miles away from the main loblolly pine forests of the southern United States. It grew its own forest of 75,000 acres. When Stephen Austin rode into southern Texas in 1821 and reached the land along the Colorado River, he recorded the scene in his saddlebag journal. *Came to the Colorado River . . . poor gravelly ridges and near the river heavy pine timber.*[1]

In 1832, Bastrop was one of the few towns in Texas. It was the southernmost town before vast stretches of unoccupied land. People camped there while scouting for land. When travelers left the town to head south, they knew they might not see a white face again. Indian attacks were frequent and violent. One man was shot through the neck while eating lunch by a spring. The Indians left, taking with them seven silver-dollar-sized pieces of his scalp. The man survived, remembering that the scalping sounded like thunder.[2]

The Indians stole the Bastrop settlers' food supplies. The settlers survived by eating the wild mustangs that grazed beside the Colorado River. They ate about one hundred in all.[3]

In 1836, the Mexican Army torched Bastrop. The settlers escaped in an event that became known as the "Runaway Scrape." But they came back, and Bastrop began to grow again.

In 1852, the *Bastrop Advertiser* was a small, failing newspaper when two teenage brothers from Mississippi purchased it. In extreme weather, the ox carts bringing paper from Houston did not make it in time for the printing deadline. Still, the *Bastrop Advertiser* always went to press on Thursday, no matter what; the brothers printed it on wrapper paper. The newspaper survived as "Texas' Oldest Weekly Newspaper Since March 1, 1853."

In 1862, fire destroyed half of the Bastrop business district. Bastrop survived, and the people replaced wooden structures with brick buildings.[4]

In 1869, when the town was already crippled by the Civil War, the Colorado River flooded it. Bastrop survived and built a wrought-iron bridge over the river in 1889.

In 1883, the Bastrop courthouse burned, but the rest of the town survived.

In 1890, a fire began in the livery stable on Main Street, killing nineteen horses. No people were killed, the fire did not spread, and Bastrop was spared.

In the next century Bastrop experienced more growth and battled less disaster. As new bridges, roads, a power plant, and a state park emerged, Bastrop began to acquire its own identity. The people realized the uniqueness of its forest of loblolly pines. The towns around Bastrop have oak trees and cacti, but not pine trees.

Even scientists are baffled about how the 75,000-acre loblolly pine forest sprang up in Bastrop, nearly eighty miles west of the main belt of similar trees. Loblolly pines stretch from East Texas to Florida, but the Bastrop pines are not a part of that main group. Were the Bastrop pines perhaps planted by birds or Native Americans? It's as if the little grove of loblollies wandered away one day, got lost, and couldn't find its way back home.

That's the image from which Bastrop chose its nickname: Home of the Lost Pines.

ESCAPE ARTIST NAMESAKE

The town of Bastrop was named after a shady figure, Baron

> de Bastrop. Having given himself a new name, Mr. Bastrop was a dramatic escape artist. He was actually Mr. Bogel, a tax collector from Holland. When he was accused of stealing tax money, he fled Holland with a price on his head. Once in America, he changed his name to Baron de Bastrop, became friends with the Spanish government, and moved to Spanish Texas. When Stephen Austin's father wanted to start the settlement that eventually became Bastrop, he found an ally in Baron de Bastrop. The baron encouraged him, spoke to the governor on his behalf, and convinced the Spaniards to let him in. When the senior Austin died, Mr. Bastrop continued to take care of his land and advise Stephen Austin, who likely had no idea that Bastrop was a wanted criminal in Holland.

In the 1900s people began to move into this pine forest. Instead of Bastrop clinging only to the Colorado River, its people ventured into the forest, building roads, subdivisions, a power plant, and a state park.

From Bastrop, two highways cut into the pine forest, forming a V to the east.[a] Highway 21 heads northeast, toward the Louisiana border and the rest of the pine forest belt. This route is roughly the same path used by pioneers heading to Texas. Sam Houston came this way. Davy Crockett came this way as he headed to the Alamo. Stephen Austin came this way with his horse and saddlebag journal. Following Highway 21 through Bastrop and across the Colorado River, the road heads west to San Antonio and the Alamo, from which Davy Crockett and his men never returned.

Highway 71 heads south to Houston and the Gulf of Mexico, probably the same route used by ox carts to bring paper to the *Bastrop Advertiser*. Following Highway 71 to the northwest leads across the Colorado River to Austin, the capital of Texas, only twenty miles away. According to Bastropians, Bastrop and Austin were the final choices for state

---

[a] See maps on last page of photo section.

capital, and Bastrop lost the campaign by only one vote.

Not far from the city of Bastrop, six thousand acres of Lost Pines became Bastrop State Park. The park sits east of Bastrop in the point of the V formed by the two highways. During the Great Depression, Franklin Roosevelt's government programs sent groups of young men to Bastrop. These unemployed men, having no money to buy their next meal, were paid thirty dollars a month to create Bastrop State Park.[5] Using local resources, they built stone cabins to match the surrounding landscape. They cut pine, oak, and cedar trees to build beams, fireplace mantles, and furniture. The stone cabins, surrounded by loblolly pine trees, appear to grow out of the rolling hills of the park. Fat stone chimneys cling to their outside walls. At night, pools of yellow light spill out of paned windows.

In the late decades of the twentieth century, subdivisions sprang up in the pine forest. Excavators cut winding roads between the tall trees along the two highways stretching away from Bastrop. Entrepreneurs mapped out subdivisions and built houses. Circle D Estates sprang up north of Highway 21, just above Bastrop State Park. Bastrop Fire Station #3 is located in this area, aptly called the Circle D Station.

Tahitian Village started just south of the park, between Highway 71 and the Colorado River. As the terrain approaches the Colorado River, the land dips and swells, rising to a cliff with a stunning view of the river and the lands beyond. Vehicles wend their way up driveways with impossibly steep grades. Backyards swallow stray kickballs in deep ravines. Above, the Lost Pines create a dreamy ceiling of swaying green needles, complete with the sweet aroma of pine rosin.

There is only one main entrance to the twelve hundred homes in Tahitian Village. This main road, Tahitian Drive, splits into a Polynesian fan of roads with Polynesian names ranging from Mala Court to Keanahalululu Lane. Perhaps the developer had a love for the South Seas, or maybe he just needed a large bank of unused names. Due to the difficulty of pronouncing some of the names, emergency personnel sometimes abandon the attempt to pronounce them and choose to spell the name instead. Bastrop Fire Station #2 is located in Tahitian Village.

The Circle D subdivision and Tahitian Village are both filled with residents who love to lift their heads to the skies. They listen to the loblollies standing in clumps, whispering in the breeze. They grow dizzy watching the clouds move above the tops of the tilting pines.

In 1934, the state of Texas formed a district to take care of six hundred miles of the Colorado River area in central Texas. They called it the LCRA, the Lower Colorado River Authority. Prohibited from taxing the people living there, the district had to operate by selling utilities such as electricity and water.

Just outside Bastrop, off Highway 21, the LCRA built a huge power plant in the middle of the loblolly forest. The LCRA sells its electricity to Bluebonnet Electric Cooperative, who then sells it to the people. Bluebonnet built and maintained the electric lines threading through the Lost Pines, powering Bastrop County.

On the other side of Bastrop, the LCRA built McKinney Roughs Nature Park, an eleven-hundred-acre park. The LCRA chose this spot outside Bastrop because in those eleven hundred acres, four different types of countryside were represented. McKinney Roughs is not just pine forest, nor just prairie. At the park you can find loblolly pines, oaks, canyons, rolling prairie, and the lazy bends of the Colorado River. There are close to eighteen miles of trails that can be hiked or explored on horseback.[6] Groups of school children come to the park for tours to learn about nature.

Together, the state park, the two highways, the two subdivisions, the power plant, and the nature park create a populated forest community. Firefighters have a special name for communities like these: a wildland-urban interface. This is an area where the forest mingles with houses—many people live beside many trees. In simple terms, a wildland-urban interface is a dangerous place for a forest fire to start because it could quickly spread to many houses.

In the 1990s, Michael Fisher, Bastrop's emergency management coordinator, came up with a new word. He called the area around Bastrop a "fire plain." He used the term to describe areas likely to experience destructive fire. Like the familiar word *floodplain,* the term *fire plain* helps educate people about the precautions they need to take while living in a wildland-urban interface.[7]

Mike Fisher sometimes wondered what would happen if there were a major fire in Bastrop. Would the people of Bastrop be resourceful, efficient, and fast enough to escape? Would they survive?

> ### TRAVELING TO BASTROP
>
> Regardless from which direction a driver comes, it's necessary to pass through quite a few miles of Texas before arriving in Bastrop. Drivers rush under overpasses decorated with cement-colored lone stars and past Texas state shapes mounted on the pillars of bridges. Ranches begin to appear on the right and left with names like Elk Meadow Game Ranch, steel gates guarding their entrances. Long, well-kept lanes appear with alternating lampposts and oak trees. One can see long barns with rusty tin roofs along with miles of barbed wire fencing between closely spaced wooden posts. An occasional oil pump bobs up and down against the background of a giant pasture.
>
> Corn nuts appear on the shelves of gas stations. Locals congregate outside the gas stations, crowding picnic tables or benches in the manner of the South. Restaurants advertise their brisket. An increasing number of barbecue joints appear, with open eating areas in keeping with Texas' mild winters. White board churches sit sedately, adorned with domed roofs and long windows. Small towns dot the highways, sporting quaint antique shops and brick walls painted with Coca-Cola murals. Across the miles certain themes emerge, giving the traveler a picture of what is typical of this vast part of the southern United States.

MORE ABOUT THE STATE OF TEXAS

The state of Texas has everything, people say. But then, there's plenty of room to have everything. The following ten states would fit inside the state of Texas: Maine, New Hampshire, Vermont, Massachusetts, Connecticut, Rhode Island, New York, Pennsylvania, Ohio, and North Carolina. Texas spans 801 miles north to south and 773 miles east to west. With a 624-mile coastline, Texas is home to sandy shores and water birds. It also has cacti, red cliffs, bluebonnets, red grapefruits, oil, prairies, and George Bush's ranch.

Texas, once its own country, has flown six flags: Spain, France, Mexico, the Texas Republic, the Confederacy, and the United States. The United States flag has enjoyed uninterrupted place for more than 150 years, but on few Texas flagpoles has it actually flown *alone*. The Texas Lone Star flag, with its broad stripes of red, white, and blue and its giant lone star, flies on almost every pole, as if to gently suggest that the state is no more American than Texan.

Texan pride is palpable. It's almost as if they have flag dyslexia and don't realize the national flag is on top of the pole. For example, most Americans, when traveling internationally, introduce themselves as being "from the United States." Texans tend to say, "I'm from Texas."

In addition, those who think that General Lee fought the last battle of the Civil War are mistaken. The last battle of the Civil War was fought in Texas. Although General Lee had surrendered a month earlier, the Confederates in Texas fought on. They fought another battle against the Union soldiers—and won.

Texas has three cities with populations of more than one million: Houston, San Antonio, and Dallas. If these three dots on the map are connected, they create a triangle in eastern Texas. Dallas is the top of the triangle near the Oklahoma border, Houston is the bottom right corner near the Gulf of Mexico, and San Antonio is the bottom left corner near the beginning of nowhere. Most of the triangle is inside the prairies and lakes region of Texas, west of the piney woods. Austin and Bastrop are in the San Antonio corner.

Austin is smaller than the three cities forming the triangle, but it's the capital. The state capitol building, over three hundred feet tall, is taller than the Capitol in Washington, D.C. When it was built in 1876, the state was poor but had one abundant resource. The construction crew was paid with three million acres of land.

TEN FAMILIES ALONG HIGHWAY 21

Dean, Debra, and the House That God Built
Dean and Debra Pahlow[a] lived near Circle D Estates, in a mobile home beneath the pines. Dubbed by Debra as the "House That God Built," the mobile home was packed with three sons and a daughter named Jorja.

Debra, a homeschool mom, part-time teacher and curriculum writer for other homeschooled students, and an unashamed Christian, was once a self-proclaimed witch. She had worked at an occult shop in the city of Austin, where she helped clients select a Greek or Roman god or goddess that fit their needs. She promoted and sold the symbolic upside-down cross. She worshipped John Lennon, his Beatles, and his music.

Her journey from disdain for God to faith in Him started about the time she and her husband purchased the run-down mobile home in the loblolly forest.

Debra had met her husband Dean when they were both living in Austin, Debra working at the occult shop. Disillusioned with the Catholicism of her youth, Debra liked the idea of studying gods and goddesses

[a] See "Principal Characters" list on page 7.

to choose the ones she could identify with the most. She soon learned to read astrological charts and predict futures. She sold herbs, crystals, incense, rocks, upside-down crosses, five-pointed Wiccan stars, charms, and anointing oils.

One day a man arrived at the shop door with a bloodied head. He said he'd been attacked by a man with a bat at the Laundromat but had thwarted the attempted robbery and escaped. From there he made his way to the shop, where he was a customer. Concerned, Debra cared for the young man, whose name was Dean, and helped him decide whether or not he should go to the hospital. As Dean and Debra became acquainted, she learned that he had been a Christian earlier, but through a series of circumstances had become angry at God and decided to run in the opposite direction.

Their friendship continued, and eventually Dean and Debra were married. Several years after their wedding, they moved their family from Austin to Bastrop. One Sunday they decided to go to church, although Debra doesn't know why she agreed to do it. They ended up attending numerous times. For four Sundays Debra sat stiffly on the church bench, inwardly rebelling against what she was hearing. The pastor seemed to be speaking truth, and for the first time, Debra saw a clear difference between truth and what she wanted to believe.

One day the pastor of the church, who knew the Pahlows were having vehicle problems, drove up in a Suburban. He got out and handed them the keys.

Stunned, the Pahlows' first thought was, *What do you want in return?* But there was no requirement.

"This is just for you," the pastor said, "so you know God is taking care of you in a practical way."

It had never occurred to Debra that God was interested in providing for her material needs as well as her spiritual ones. For the first time, she began to realize that God cared about the everyday details of her life as well as the condition of her soul.

As she continued to doubt her determination to reject Christianity, something began to irritate her increasingly. From the beginning, her husband had insisted on keeping an old King James Bible in their bedroom. She knew that to be consistent with what she said she believed, she had to be the gracious liberal who was okay with everything—but it still bothered her that he would not get rid of the Bible. Yet he insisted on keeping it.

Debra's mental frustration escalated until it grew too great to bear. One night she had a bitter fight with Dean. In the course of their argument, she grabbed the Bible. "Why have you been carrying this for six years?" she demanded.

"Even though it ticks me off to admit it, this book is the truth," Dean spouted. "It's just up to you what you're going to do with it." With that, he stalked out of the room.

Debra stared at the empty doorway in shock. He really thought the Bible spoke the truth? So he was deliberately ignoring it and turning away from God. *Are we just playing a meaningless game?* she thought.

The pastor's recent sermons resounded in her mind. Suddenly, she was faced with a terrifying choice. If she accepted Christianity and the God of the Bible, she would have to deny everything she had embraced and the persona she had created for herself. She would have to follow that God. It would mean turning from her Greek and Roman gods, her occult practices, and even her love for John Lennon. Lennon had become her savior, and she knew God would not allow an idol like that in her life.

What was her other option, now that she was considering that Christianity was the truth? *I will live a lie and know that I'm living a lie every day of my life. Can I handle that? No, I can't.*

It was at this time that Dean and Debra bought the mobile home on Alum Creek Drive. The house became part of their journey of faith. The journey was aided by several key people: their hospitable neighbors, Howard and Holly, as well as the congregation at the small white church on the other side of Highway 21.

The pastor and his wife, who lived beside the church, became mentors for the Pahlows. Debra found the pastor's wife inspiring in her journey to faith in God. She had become handicapped at a young age, partially paralyzed by a sudden attack of multiple sclerosis. However, she spoke of her many blessings: the blessing of energy, the blessing of a handy scooter to ride, and the blessing of not needing much medication. She was grateful for the Bible and often mentioned the book of James, which warns that Christians should expect trials.

With this encouragement and support, Debra put aside the upside-down cross. Instead, she displayed a metal-work cross crafted by one of the homeschooled students in her one-day academy classes. Behind the cross, swirls of metal circled like a hurricane. "Mrs. Pahlow, this is what they call the 'Eye of the Storm,' " the student had told her. The cross drew the eye to itself, the resting place in the middle of the commotion.

The Pahlows' backyard was filled with pine trees as well as one small oak twenty-five feet from the back door of the mobile home. Hanging from the oak tree by a nylon rope was a plastic swing shaped like a pickle. The green pickle swing had belonged to Dean since he was three years old. Its fat plastic body now boosted the Pahlow children high into the air.

Itsatown and the Gibbons Family
Michael and Shirley Gibbons also lived off Highway 21 northeast of Bastrop. Mike was once a firefighter. With Cherokee Indian heritage, Mike was the master of many skills. He had his own windmill, and it pumped water into a 20,000-gallon tank. The windmill fed a solar-powered water heater that supplied the outdoor shower with warm water if the electricity went out.

Mike's most prized possession was the Gibbons family museum. Christened "Itsatown," the museum was housed in an outbuilding beside Mike's house. Visitors reached it by walking through a network of wooden and chain-link metal gates, through stretches of grass that sometimes fed long-horned cattle, and past Mike's windmill. The wooden door of Itsatown opened with a squeak.

Itsatown had a small library, and on its shelves was a book called *Stalking the Wild Asparagus*. This book about surviving on wild foods was written by Mike's grandfather, Euell Gibbons. The Gibbons family was noted for being able to survive without modern conveniences. Once, Mike and his grandfather survived for two months in a wilderness, eating only wild foods.

Itsatown included a doll and teddy bear room, an antique bathroom with a window full of blue glass pieces, a booth named the Longhorn Café, a blacksmith shop, a silver shop, a saddle shop, and a trading post. The trading post was filled with moccasins, leather-fringed jackets, and beadwork made by the Gibbons family.

All the rooms reflected Mike's skills, some of which he learned at a Quaker school in Iowa. He had been sent there by his grandfather after being expelled from high school for his outbursts of temper. The Quaker school did not have a sports program, so they put their money into their art program. Mike grew familiar with silversmithing, glassblowing, metal sculpting, blacksmithing, and pottery. At different times in his life, he'd been a plumber, journeyman pipefitter, high-rise welder, and firefighter. He was now employed as a paramedic.

The name *Itsatown* came from a visiting child who looked around the museum and exclaimed to his mother, "It's a town!"

If disaster were ever to strike, the Gibbons family would be far better prepared than most people to live without modern conveniences.

Retired Missionaries—Wesley and Margaret Peschke
Wesley and Margaret Peschke lived on the other side of Highway 21. Like Mike Gibbons, Wesley built most of what he owned.

Wesley had a talent. He could notice something—anything—and come home, draw plans for it, and then build it. Once he had made a lamp out of an old electric meter. When the lamp was turned on, the meter ran.

Wesley had constructed a small building, open to the air like a gazebo.

From a local recycling plant, he collected ten thousand green glass bottles. After washing each green bottle by hand, he mortared them with their necks meeting in the middle of the wall so that the round bottoms of the bottles appeared as circles to the inside and outside, like a well-designed pattern of polka dots.

Wesley also built their house. He wanted a house with character—one he could build with his own hands and observe with satisfaction at the end. In 1978 he drew up the plans and began to build on Saturdays. Special pieces, like the fireplace made of stalactites and stalagmites, were ordered. Wesley and Margaret special-ordered a front wall made of native stone. The entrance hallway leading up to the fireplace was also made from polished stalactites and stalagmites from a Texan cave that had been discovered during road-building.

In 1985, after seven years of Saturday work had finished the house, Wesley and Margaret moved in around their thirtieth anniversary. They went out to dinner to celebrate with some friends, and then they met for dessert and a dedication at the Peschkes' newly completed house.

The trees set the tone. Pecans hung from a tree just outside the dining room window. There were more pecan trees in the backyard, but Wesley and Margaret did not harvest them since the blackbirds and squirrels always took off with them before they were ripe. Fruit trees dotted the backyard as well. The pine trees had grown tall and breezy, casting cool shade over the bottle house and the other outbuildings.

But Margaret's real treasures were in the house. When Wesley went on mission trips to build houses in Central America, he often brought home souvenirs. Margaret loved antiques and collectibles, like the painting of an Indian made with black paint and real gold leaf. Her great-grandmother had been Amish, and Margaret now owned the Amish bonnet and washstand once belonging to her matriarch. To that she added Wesley's souvenirs: rice china from Panama and clay pottery, lamps, and tablecloths from Honduras, Haiti, and Mexico. The Kuna Indians produced molas, intricate wall hangings best described as reverse appliqué. Wesley framed the molas, and they were carefully hung in a place of honor on the wall.

Many of these items found places on the twenty-one-foot shelves of the living room, near the pictures of Wesley and Margaret when they were dating and the cake topper from their wedding.

In 2003 Margaret photographed her entire house of antiques and souvenirs, just in case there would be a fire. She took the photos to a safe deposit box at her bank in Bastrop.

While in Bastrop, she and Wesley would often stop at their favorite restaurant, Maxine's on Main. At Maxine's, beverages came in quart jars. Wesley would order his favorite vegetable plates, choosing from sweet potato with praline sauce, okra, corn casserole, and other tasty choices.

AN EXPERIENCE FOR THE PALATE

The city of Bastrop is home to unique and tasty food options. Lock Drug Store operates a soda fountain that has been going since 1905. Besides, they offer a stunning menu of ice cream with names like *Southern Style Blackberry Cobbler*, which can be eaten on a high stool in front of the original marble bar.

Outside the city center, Billy's Pit Bar-B-Q advertises "Need No Teeth to Eat Our Beef" on the side of napkin holders plopped on brown folding tables without cloths. Diners order barbecue or beef brisket at a long table, where workers skillfully slice the beef against the grain into Texas-style strips. Diners then take their seats in the dining area, under the watchful gaze of fourteen deer mounts on the walls above. Also tacked on the walls are awards from the *Bastrop Advertiser.*

REMEMBERING THE PAST

Like Wesley and Margaret's house, the Bastrop of today is hard to distinguish from the Bastrop of history, because

> history is a central feature of the city. Bastropians love antiques, and in a sense the city itself is an antique. Bastrop was once a stop on El Camino Real (the Royal Road) that stretched from Mexico to Louisiana. El Camino Real was the road that kept Texas alive in the early years, and it cut right through Bastrop.
>
> Chestnut Street now traces that path and is dotted with commemorative medallions that bring back the past. The medallions cemented into the sidewalk are the shape and color of giant pennies, but each is engraved differently with an important moment or monument in Bastrop's history. There's a medallion for the *Bastrop Advertiser*, a medallion for Bastrop's three bridges, and a medallion for the fire of 1862.

Patty Timmons

Patty Timmons lived in the north end of the Circle D area, with her husband, a dog named Shadow, and numerous cats.

Patty had a scrapbook with pictures of her father, who raised her until he was killed in an accident when Patty was ten years old. From there, Patty's life consisted of moving from relative to relative. Through each move, Patty clung to her scrapbook with the photos of her father and the grandparents she had never met. She stored it in a safe place in her house.

Patty loved crafting sun catchers with metal wire and colored gems. She knew the names of the various stones and what their colors symbolized, which gave meaning to her artwork.

Adam and Cindy Cruz

Adam and Cindy Cruz lived in a house with rock walls on Cardinal Drive in Circle D. They had been married for seventeen years. It had been about five years since they had become Christians. Cindy's family did not appreciate their new Christianity. After Cindy's conversion, if her family wanted to party and drink alcohol, they would simply not invite her. Even though her mother was Catholic, she did not know Jesus as Cindy had learned to know Him.

Cindy had a history of health problems, including chronic back pain. The extreme weather in Texas was difficult for her. Still, she was grateful for the many times God had healed her.

Nicholas Cowey
Nicholas Cowey worked at McKinney Roughs Nature Park on the west side of Bastrop, but he and his wife lived in the pines on the east side, in the Circle D area. At his job, Nicholas gave tours to students and told them about the plants and animals native to this area of Texas. He also taught history lessons for school children, using costumes and accessories appropriate to the lesson: coonskin caps, old uniforms, and ancient guns.

During the years of the two hundredth anniversary of Lewis and Clark's exploration trip, Nicholas led groups of boys in the steps of the explorers, teaching them Christian leadership along with adventure. He showed them an original peace medal, the coins with George Washington's imprint that the explorers gave to the Indians to introduce them to their "new father." Nicholas turned to his collection of forty Lewis and Clark books for interesting facts and ideas for the trips.

His house in the Lost Pines stored his many props and collectibles. Nicholas had three insect cabinets full of preserved butterflies, dragonflies, and beetles. The cabinets also held arrowheads and lichen samples. He had 40 period costumes, 350 animal furs, microscopes, telescopes, a reed organ from the 1890s, 62 pieces of cast iron, and 4,000 books.

Nicholas built a miniature log cabin for Ranger, his half-Boxer, half-Pyrenees dog. He and Ranger were great friends.

Nicholas and his wife dreamt of having children and homeschooling them. The loblolly pine forest was the perfect setting for nature lovers wanting to homeschool their children. However, they were still in the waiting stage for that dream to be realized. Following a miscarriage in 2011, the couple knew they had to exercise patience and faith. They worked through their grief by reading the book of Job, a story of great suffering.

Efrain and Debi Canava

Efrain and Debi Canava moved to their Bastrop home because they were attracted to the trees. Their property stood between two roads, but they couldn't see either one because the trees were so thick. The ravines, creeks, roads, and even the other houses in the Circle D area were hidden by the trees.

They lived in a two-story log home. Debi's brothers and sisters gave her the most valuable family possession, the family Bible, because they believed it would be safest with her at the log cabin in the woods.

Efrain had a special possession as well—one that didn't take up much space. It was a handwritten note from his father, a man he never remembers meeting. Efrain's father died when Efrain was a baby, only forty days old.

Alan Donaldson

Asian souvenirs and books packed Alan Donaldson's house. His parents, who lived in occupied Japan after World War II, provided the Asian souvenirs. Alan would have been born in Asia had his parents not decided to fly back to the States just before he was born. As it was, he was delivered in North Carolina by emergency C-section, making him a native of the United States only. When Alan grew up, his parents told him they had almost named him Donald MacDonald Donaldson.

"Cooler heads prevailed," Alan tells his friends wryly.

His grandfather returned from a trip to Italy once, bringing him a 1649 edition of Euclid's geometry. Inside the cover, it had a special stamp saying that it was identical to the valuable copy kept secure in the Vatican in Italy. Swords, guns, gold coins, and an Egyptian scarab beetle competed for attention with his hundreds of books.

Alan enjoyed reading, and he would usually have two books he was working on at the same time. One he dubbed his "restaurant book," which he would take with him to read while waiting for his order. The other was his "home book," which he would read at home.

Although he was a voracious reader, Alan enjoyed the hard physical labor and the adrenaline of fighting fires. He was a volunteer firefighter, living minutes away from Bastrop's Station #3, the Circle D Station.

René and Kathy Rizk
René Rizk had lived in the United States for more than half his life and owned a busy mechanic shop on the main artery of road between Austin and Bastrop. He and his wife, Kathy, had two sons. The oldest son had two children, a preschool girl and an infant son. The little girl loved to visit Grandpa's house.

The younger son lived at home. The Rizks had been remodeling and improving their home in the forest for about twelve years. In 2011 they had just finished a small addition for their son's part of the house.

About thirty-five years before, in 1976, René lived with his mother in Lebanon. He was twenty-one years old at the time. The Middle East in 1976 had much the same tone as in 2011. Muslims and Christians and Jews were all fighting madly over ancient differences that nobody could resolve.

Lebanon was particularly flammable. In 1976 it burst into the flames of civil war. It was at this point, with the noise of gunfire reaching their house, that René and his mother fled to the coast. There they took a small boat to the island of Cyprus, where by some miracle they were issued green cards in two weeks. They wasted no time heading to the United States.

Between running his busy mechanic shop, remodeling, and doting on his grandchildren, René didn't waste a lot of time thinking about his escape from disaster. He was just glad it was far in the past.

Bill and Patsy Ludwig
Bill and Patsy Ludwig lived on a lot with 370 trees. They were huge trees, taller and stronger than the pines and oaks in closely packed

forests. There were hundreds of oaks and pines, plus five cedars.

In a shed out back, Bill and Patsy stored their treasures: an old carousel horse, antique trains, vintage dolls, and four antique pedal cars they were saving for their grandchildren.

They also stored irreplaceable family treasures. Bill's grandfather had been a skillful artist, and Bill had a number of his watercolor paintings. Bill also inherited collections of stamps and coins from his father.

Bill and Patsy had bought their house from gypsies who never paid their income taxes. When the gypsies ran out of money, they went to New Orleans to tell fortunes. They always carried large purses with them to stock up on anything free: shampoo in hotels or candy at the bank. They had painted the house and outbuildings bright pink. Bill and Patsy repainted the buildings.

Patsy could not relate to people like the gypsies, who were content to live with cockroaches and humiliate themselves by taking suitcases of free things. Patsy did understand poverty, however. She remembered living with her grandmother as a child, surviving on pancakes and homemade sugar syrup toward the end of each month. But her grandmother had insisted that there was no excuse for being dirty, because soap was cheap.

Patsy also understood disaster. She had lived through a flood in Pittsburgh and a hurricane in Florida. She knew how it felt to be the one who needed help. Perhaps that was why she was soft-hearted. People sometimes told her it was a fault.

But Patsy was not ashamed of her compassion. It enabled her to relate well to children, and she had worked as a kindergarten and first-grade teacher. She also had a special touch with animals. Bill came home from a trip to Oklahoma one time and discovered an abandoned kitten, days old, in the back of his truck. Patsy named it Daisy May and nursed it back to health, feeding it every two hours until it was independent.

Patsy regularly gave money to people less fortunate, always saving part of her check to give to needy family members. Some people told her that she was being used. Patsy pondered this as she wondered how she could tell if someone was truly poor or just lazy. Sometimes it was hard to tell.

But her compassion made her want to help, no matter whether people totally deserved it or not.

3

FOUR FAMILIES ALONG HIGHWAY 71

Larry Miller

A small back road turned north off Highway 71. Larry Miller's farm was off this road to the right. Larry's farm included nine barns, eight hundred acres, tractors, and goats. One of his favorite buildings was his shed, where he kept his mounted animals, including a prize sailfish. In the building he also stored his forty-year collection of tools and an aluminum riverboat. Although his career job was working on trains, traveling from station to station across Texas, his farm could have been called a job as well.

As a hobby, Larry raised goats for many years, specialty goats that won prizes in shows and were worth up to ten thousand dollars.

When Larry stood at the edge of his pasture and called the goats, the brown and white animals came running, bleating with eagerness, pounding past the gnarled oak trees in their domain. The bouncing herd mingled into a mass of horns, pink and green numbered tags, flopping brown ears, and smooth white bodies, but Larry could pick out his favorites with a quick glance.

Larry traveled two hundred miles to buy high-quality goat feed. He bought Anatolian guard dogs imported from Turkey to protect the herd from the local mountain lions that prowled the Colorado River bluffs not far away. Larry had once owned a racehorse and lost it to a mountain lion.

Larry's wife sometimes told him that he was obsessed with his goats, their genetics, their feed, and their protection. She teased him about needing rehab. However, unlike most activities that require rehab, Larry's hobby was a business. And why not buy good-quality goats? "It costs the same to feed a good one as a sorry one," Larry pointed out.

Jimmy Mack

Jimmy Mack and his wife were world travelers, but their home was in Bastrop on Tall Forest Drive, south of Highway 71.

The world traveling began with Jimmy's career as a parachute tester. He had his first jump at the age of sixteen. By his three thousandth jump, he still thought it was fun. He admitted that the second jump was scarier than the first, but there was always an emergency parachute to activate if the main one didn't engage. Working for the parachute company, Jimmy flew to factories all over the world, demonstrating new parachutes and training employees how to pack them.

After quitting that job, Jimmy and his wife kept traveling. They celebrated his fiftieth birthday on the Nile River in Egypt. In 2011 Jimmy was on the Geek Squad at Best Buy, working with computers and traveling whenever he was able.

Jimmy grew up outside Philadelphia, but like so many others, he loved Bastrop because of the pine trees. Living under the trees was like living in a resort. Despite all his travels, Jimmy admitted to himself that sometimes it was hard to go on vacation. On windy days, the pine forest sounded like the ocean. There weren't many places as beautiful as home.

George Martinez

George Martinez was born in Austin, thirty miles from Bastrop. For years he worked as an electrical engineer.

In 2011, George and his wife and two sons lived in a comfortable house in Tahitian Village, the subdivision with deep ravines, steep roads, and names with difficult pronunciations. They had a back patio perfect for grilling and eating outside, unless the Texas sun became so hot that even the patio umbrella's shade offered little relief.

George, a volunteer firefighter, lived minutes away from Station #2, the Tahitian Village Station. The front glass door of the station proudly sported the insignia of a pine tree surrounded by a ring of blue and gold. The doors of all the department trucks were adorned with the same logo.

Dangerous or not, everyone in Bastrop loved the Lost Pines.

Ryan Terranova

A young man named Ryan Terranova lived at the mouth of Tahitian Village in 2011. He worked for his mother at the Tahitian Village Market, a brick gas station with a small deli. Outside, tables and chairs and a bulletin board of announcements and business cards invited customers to linger.

Ryan had a red minivan he named Betsy. For a while, he and Betsy offered a taxi service, driving elderly people to low-cost pharmacies in Houston. Betsy now had 256,000 miles behind her. She had had some surgery and her engine had been rebuilt. Mechanically, she worked well, but Ryan worried that his minivan would fall apart someday.

Tahitian Drive, the only official way to enter and exit Tahitian Village, was the road that separated Ryan's apartment from the market. Although there were hidden back roads, most of the residents of the twelve hundred houses in Tahitian Village used the main exit.

4

THE HOT SUMMER

The summer of 2011 was torturously hot in Bastrop, Texas. There was almost no rain.

The firefighters and local officials made rules. "No campfires! No grilling! Burn ban in effect!" Some of the rules had already been in place since the fall of 2010. The winter rains were not enough to soften the drought. In the summer of 2011, the sun rose hot, day after day after day. For ninety days in a row, the temperature reached one hundred degrees or higher.

The sun beat down on Fire Station #1 in downtown Bastrop. It heated a cast iron firefighter standing on a brick pedestal in front of the fire station. He stood in a partially collapsed doorway with an ax in his right hand and a small child in his left. The statue grew so hot it seemed as though he really had just stepped from a burning building.

Chief Henry Perry kept a close watch on the weather. More than two years had passed since February 2009, when the Wilderness Ridge Fire had spread across 1,491 acres and destroyed twenty-six homes and twenty businesses. Texas Forest Service dedicated a twenty-nine-page case study to this fire, entitled "Wilderness Ridge Fire, Bastrop County: The Most Destructive Wildfire in Central Texas." The abstract notes the conditions that preceded the wildfire:

> Drought conditions, extremely dry and windy weather, and a small spark all came together to form the devastating wildfire. Sparks from downed power lines ignited the Wilderness Ridge Fire, the most destructive wildfire in Central Texas. Fuels were critically dry due to the entrenched drought that was present across Central Texas.[1]

In the summer of 2011, the drought was even more severe, and the temperatures were higher than in February 2009. The Bastrop Fire Department had been busy ever since Wilderness Ridge Fire, responding to 850 fire calls in 2010. The Bastrop firefighters didn't want another Wilderness Ridge.

> The people who work with wildfire are like lion tamers, attempting to control an extremely powerful and unpredictable force of nature. And as lion tamers do, they need to learn as much as they can about what they are trying to restrain.[2]

Almost all the Bastrop firefighters were volunteers, but they were well-trained to fight wildfires, knowing that the Bastrop area was prone to them. Fighting a wildland fire was more complex than fighting a house fire. Firefighters needed special training so that no one would get hurt and damage could be minimized.

Sitting in his office at Bastrop Fire Station #1, with the welcome relief of air conditioning, Chief Henry Perry placed a bag of pecans on his desk to symbolize a structure fire. He surrounded the pecans with office supplies (a stapler and Post-it note stacks) to symbolize fire trucks. He taught that a structure fire was simple to surround and soak with water. Even if the structure were destroyed, the cooling water might save some of the possessions inside.

Not so with a forest fire. There is no way to surround a forest fire. In many cases firefighters are told to wait for a forest fire to come to them. They are trained to build fire lines by removing fuel from the ground so that the fire is forced to stop when it reaches their boundary line. Fire trucks are parked in a safe area with lots of empty space and little fuel. This open space, where a fire cannot reach, is called *defensible space*.

> ## THE DROUGHT MAP
> On the colored drought map for 2011, severe drought was recorded with a dark purple color. Less intense drought areas were colored red and orange. In March 2011, most of Texas was orange. Then it began to be shaded red, then purple. By June, a majority of Texas was the severe purple color. By August, except for a small red nose at the southernmost tip of Texas, the entire state was purple, and the dark dye on the map had bled into New Mexico, Colorado, Oklahoma, Kansas, and Louisiana. Above them, the Dakotas and Montana were colored the dark green of "extremely moist."[3]

The sun beat down on Highway 21, an avenue of loblolly pines angling northeast out of Bastrop, toward the main belt of Lost Pines miles away. It heated the metal guard rails until they weren't safe to touch.

It scorched Bastrop State Park lying between Highways 21 and 71. The sun scared away many campers in the summer of 2011. It reflected off the panes of glass in the Depression-era stone cabins. It burned the skin of bikers on the park's extensive biking paths. Its effects kept the small group of campers warm even at night, so there was no need for the forbidden campfires.

The campers who did brave the heat found that Bastrop State Park was still beautiful, even in a drought. Every photo they took was framed by the rough patterned trunks of the loblolly pines and the shadows of whispering green branches. The overhead branches turned biking trails into tunnels of piney green. When night fell over the park and the pines darkened against the Texan sky, yellow light glowed through the windows of the stone cabins.

The sun sizzled Lake Bastrop, lying north of the highway like a silvery water creature, its tentacles stretching into the surrounding countryside. The power plant beside Lake Bastrop radiated with heat as it sat off the lake like a beached cruise ship full of chemicals. The Bluebonnet Electric Cooperative power poles and electric lines grew hot as they stretched away from the plant, cutting sharp easement paths through the loblolly pine forest. The easements, always kept free of trees, cut the forest into neat polygons as they guided the power lines to their destinations.

The firefighters were not the only ones watching the hot summer. Bluebonnet Electric Cooperative was forced to charge record-high electricity bills.

Along Highway 21, the Bluebonnet power lines brought electricity to Dean and Debra Pahlow's mobile home from God, Mike and Shirley Gibbons' Itsatown (which barely needed electricity, thanks to his windmill), Wesley and Margaret's self-made home and electric-meter lamp, Patty Timmons' home at the top of Circle D, Adam and Cindy's house with rock walls, Nicholas Cowey's house full of historical supplies and natural artifacts, Efrain and Debi's log cabin with the family Bible, Alan Donaldson's house full of books and Asian souvenirs, René Rizk's newly-remodeled house, and Bill and Patsy's home surrounded by 370 tall trees. Along Highway 71, heading southeast to Houston, the lines brought power to Tahitian Village's twelve hundred homes and Fire Station #3.

Bluebonnet's electricity powered the city of Bastrop itself, the gray section on the map where Highways 21 and 71 come together. The electricity flowed to the griddles at Maxine's on Main, where the cooks fried griddle cakes twelve inches wide, dropping blueberries into the batter one by one to prevent smashing. The power ran to Bastrop Station #1, the main station where Chief Henry Perry sat at his desk against a background of fire hats, mugs, and fat binders. Bluebonnet's electricity powered the presses at the *Bastrop Advertiser,* where Mike Gibbons' wife Shirley worked, and the white block Bastrop Library perched above the Colorado River. It powered the bank, where Margaret Peschke kept her house photos in a safe deposit box, as well as Best Buy, where Jimmy Mack worked on computers. It powered René Rizk's mechanic shop west of town and the LCRA's McKinney Roughs Nature Park where Nicholas Cowey talked about the wonders of creation.

"It's been a long summer and, with at least a few more weeks of above-normal highs ahead of us, it's important to conserve energy and save money when you can," said Bluebonnet's CEO in an August 26 news release. Bluebonnet promised to do what they could to work with people struggling to pay their high bills in heat conditions where turning the air conditioner off might not be safe.

As the sun hovered over Dean and Debra's house from God, the plastic pickle swing softened. The oak tree from which the pickle swing hung, as well as the taller surrounding pines, dried out. The Pahlows' backyard trampoline grew even more supple with the heat.

On quiet nights Debra would lie on her back on the still-warm trampoline, looking up at the nodding heads of the loblolly pines and staring dreamily at the stars resting like colossal tiaras on the heads of the swaying pines. On those quiet nights staring at the stars, Debra reflected on the past.

She remembered how the mobile home in the cul-de-sac and her faith in God came about the same time, and God built both together. As He had built a home out of a house full of holes and German cockroaches, He built a woman of faith out of a witch who could read tarot cards and deliver spells.

Debra recalled the day, driving into the Alum Creek cul-de-sac, when she promised herself that she would not live here—the area was full of run-down houses. And then, a few months later, signing the papers that made her and Dean owners of the back lot, the one with the skirtless single-wide mobile home with its pipes exposed. The one with the junk carpeting the backyard as if someone had opened the back door and shoved the garbage out for years.

She remembered the men from their new church helping Dean build cabinets, lay carpet, and patch holes. The plumbing and wiring were a mess and had to be redone, but the pastor, being an electrician, pitched in.

She recalled the church women helping her sift through the backyard: car hoods mixed with lamps and vases that covered broken bottles and diapers.

The back door had been just a thin interior door screwed into the door frame to keep people from exiting and plummeting four feet straight to the ground.

She remembered moving in, sharing a bedroom with their three sons. She remembered cooking without a stove, serving instant oatmeal and toaster oven meals until the needed repairs could be made.

Recalling the years without air conditioning and the days when she was certain it was hotter inside the mobile home than out, Debra remembered thinking, *God, help us.* She was too embarrassed about their plight to invite herself and her family over to someone else's house. But her faithful church friend and neighbor Holly would call often from her air-conditioned house. "You want to come over for burgers tonight?" she would ask.

Debra would reply enthusiastically and fling the phone down almost before Holly could say goodbye. Then she would grab the children and head to Holly's house.

She remembered the winters being just the opposite. "This is like *Little House on the Prairie,*" Debra encouraged her children when they found the rare Texan snow actually drifting into the house. All they had were space heaters, so Debra often went to bed wearing gloves and a scarf, bundling herself in a blanket to be able to sleep. Their little beta fish even froze one night and was remembered as a "fish popsicle."

Even though the house was "uninsurable," she and Dean had

continued to repair and upgrade over the next years, as God provided for them. Staring up at the tops of the pines during the 2011 summer evenings with the sun mercifully off duty, Debra reflected that, whatever the house had been, there was one thing it had not been: dull. The trailer from God was like an uncharted adventure.

Over and over she had poured her heart out to God. "I've got nothing," she had said. "I don't know what to do." Always, there was an answer. The carload of food. The American Indian who showed up around Easter with a ham. The kind friend who had paid for bug treatments to get rid of the German cockroaches when they barely had money to buy food.

The house that God built was the place Debra had learned that God was always faithful. He had always provided—not so much that they would forget God, but not so little that they couldn't make it.

Across the road, the sun heated the little white church and the parsonage where the pastor and his wife lived since 2000. The small multi-purpose outbuilding became stuffy. The pastor used it as an office, a library for his many books, and a gallery of his deceased great-uncle's watercolors. The smothering heat reached the little log cabin where the pastor's ninety-year-old uncle carved wooden bowls and candlesticks.

As Mike Gibbons came and went from his 24-hour paramedic shifts with the ambulance service, the hot sun evaporated water from his 20,000-gallon tank and warmed the windmill that pumped the water. The solar-powered water heater received lots of energy to provide warm showers. The longhorns grazed in a nearly grassless pasture.

The heat threatened the family heirlooms inside Itsatown. It scorched the red letters that spelled "Itsatown" above the museum door. Heat rays beat against the collection of blue glass lined in the window of the antique bathroom. The trading post room with the handmade family moccasins, cradle-boards, powder horns, and leather boots became suffocating, as did the saddle shop with its collection of furs and saddlebags and its sample board of thirty-two kinds of barbed wires.

The antique Western Union telegrams and World War II sugar coupons dried out. The rusted kerosene lamp hanging from a nail above the Longhorn Café heated until it seemed ready to ignite itself. The heat seeped into the pages of *Stalking the Wild Asparagus* and the other books in the library.

Mike had installed an air conditioner in the room with the most chance of heat damage: the doll and teddy bear room. The window unit worked overtime in the summer of 2011 to protect the hundreds of dolls in Mike's mother's collection: Raggedy Ann dolls, Cabbage Patch dolls, life-sized dolls, historical figure dolls, and Indian dolls. There were dolls with crocheted dresses, dolls in lacey gowns and bonnets, and dolls with yarn hair. Some dolls had ribbons, some had gingham dresses, and some had painted yellow curls. Bears with tennis shoes, bears with colored scarves, and bears with hats sat softly around the room.

As the summer wore on, the price of hay rose. Mike realized he might have to sell his long-horned cattle, which had already eaten all the available grass.

The usually cool bottle house in Wesley and Margaret Peschke's backyard became so hot that it was no longer enjoyable to have a picnic within its glass walls. Through the bottles embedded in mortar, the hot sun glowed green.

Wesley had planted the garden with green beans, tomatoes, corn, radishes, and asparagus. He had placed tin around the garden to keep the rabbits out. As the garden scorched and the tin toasted, the heat radiated into his little greenhouse. The new chickens that Wesley had bought became stressed from the heat. The pear tree dried up, the pecan trees browned, and the sticky rosin in the pines heated up.

Margaret had insisted on four exterior doors when their house was built. If there was ever a fire, she wanted exit routes. "I just thought it was a smart thing to do, living in the woods like this," Margaret said. "I wanted a way out."

They had made their house special. Bastrop's own cedar lined the bathroom walls, and a spacious deck wrapped around the back of the house. Margaret perched a decorative red tricycle on the front step. Her favorite oak tree grew close to the kitchen window. She would look out at this tree time and again and say, "Oh, God, you're so good to us."

At Patty Timmons' house on Sage Road, at the top of Circle D, the heat made all the residents of the household irritable and exhausted. The dog, Shadow, languished in the heat, and the cats became even lazier than usual. Patty's sunflowers and garden tools roasted. Her metal outdoor furniture became too hot to lounge on, even for the cats. Patty's scrapbook with pictures of the father she had only known as a young girl was stored in an air-conditioned room, safely away from the heat.

Nicholas Cowey tried to stay cool as he guided tours at McKinney Roughs Nature Park on the west side of Bastrop. The sun superheated the inside of his vehicle, exhausting him as he drove through Bastrop to his house on the east side of the pine forest. The little log cabin Nicholas had built for his dog, Ranger, gave shelter from the sun, but even the shade was hot.

In the midst of the thick forest and brush that separated them from the two roads beside their property, Efrain and Debi Canava tried in vain to stay cool in their log cabin. They had an elderly neighbor who had a metal gate in front of his property. During the summer, the gate became dangerous to lean against, burning any skin that touched it.

When Alan Donaldson suited up in fire gear at Bastrop Station #3 in Circle D, he felt nearly smothered. The sun scorched him when he went to work. When he went out to eat, the sun threatened to warp the "restaurant book" in his passenger seat.

Alan had been with the fire department for six years. Earlier in the hot summer of 2011, the Bastrop firefighters battled a wildfire that burned more than one thousand acres but no houses. Alan didn't mind fighting it, but sometimes the night stretched late as he stood guard on the fire line. When the battle became exhausting, Alan would look up and see the stars high above the hot, dark earth that smelled like burning grass. The stars, twinkling back at him, inspired him to keep on fighting the fire. At least when the sky held stars instead of the sun, the heat was less intense.

At René Rizk's mechanic shop on Highway 71, east of Bastrop, the sun baked through the windshields of the cars waiting to be repaired. It turned the mechanics' bays into suffocating caves during the heat of the day.

Like Nicholas Cowey, René worked on the west side of town and lived on the east side of town. Their newly remodeled house in the woods insulated René and his family from the worst of the heat.

On Bill and Patsy Ludwig's land with 370 tall trees, the sun bleached the buildings and the shed with the four pedal cars. It threatened to melt off the paint and reveal the alarming bright pink coats applied by the purse-carrying gypsies. Inside the house, the watercolor paintings done by Bill's grandfather were safe from the sun.

Inside the pines and cedars full of oil and rosin, temperatures continued to rise. Because it did not cool down much at night and no moisture was returned to the tree, the pine needle oil continued to grow hotter and hotter. Although the air temperature was near 100 degrees, the oils, sap, rosin, and tar in the pine needles rose to 120 degrees.

Trees that stay green all year, like Bill and Patsy's pines and cedars, are extra flammable because they contain more oil than trees that lose their leaves in the fall. Since the right amount of heat for rosin to vaporize is 140 degrees, their trees and all the Lost Pines were only 20 degrees away from becoming clouds of flammable gas.

Larry's prize goats bleated as they searched for grass. The shed that housed his mounted animals became an oven. As Larry rode across Texas on trains, he saw brown everywhere. The same radiant heat was present wherever he went, drying up the prairies and oaks and cacti.

From their home on Tall Forest Drive, Jimmy Mack and his wife plotted their next traveling venture that summer. The heat oppressed Jimmy as he traveled to and from his Geek Squad job at Best Buy, where he pulled open laptops instead of parachutes. The heat burst on him with suffocating force when he stepped out of Maxine's diner after his morning coffee with a table full of friends.

Jimmy and his friends came for coffee every morning. Maxine's was like a home away from home—so much so that the men sometimes forgot to tip. They would sit around the table beside the wall map of the Colorado River, discussing politics, the price of sorghum, the group member who dented his truck by backing into a pole, or the downfall of the economy. The hottest topic in late summer concerned Texas Governor Rick Perry's announcement that he would join the 2012 presidential race. With their work clothes, plaid button-downs, and cowboy hats, the group of men looked like pioneers whose campfire was a table at Maxine's.

In the 1960s someone had put a Laundromat and Western Union office into the restaurant building. But later, Jimmy's friend Tommy Hoover, also sitting at the table for morning coffee, had restored the building to near-original condition. He had removed the extra rooms as well as the ceiling, revealing the beautiful timber of the original roof beams, stamped *Houston*.

TOMMY HOOVER, RESTORER OF OLD BUILDINGS

Tommy Hoover is the man behind many of the old restored buildings seen around Bastrop. Since he and his wife reworked their first home many years ago, he can count sixty-five restorations in which he's been involved. Some of them were restorations of the buildings on Bastrop's Main Street. Others were buildings that he moved from other locations, clustering them in subdivisions or small plazas. Tommy would keep his eyes open for old buildings that seemed to be in the way or were about to be torn down. After making the purchase, he would hire a crew to move the house, which occasionally meant lowering the roof or cutting the building in half for the move.

One building he found was an old church that had been turned into a feed barn and was used for storing hay. Tommy moved it to a historic village in Bastrop on the bluffs just above the Colorado River. It is now Olde World Bakery, a pleasant café and coffee shop that serves authentically-shaped scones. The scones are round like they are in Scotland, not triangular like American scones. To the village, he added a general store, a one-room school, and an old scale house from Texas' cotton days. The general store had been stacked with lumber, which he was able to use for further renovating as well as building porches for the other houses in the village. The general store became a restaurant, its glass-paneled windows looking out over the waters of the Colorado. When the ceiling was redone, Tommy instructed the workers to pay no attention to the color of the boards. Consequently, the ceiling became an eclectic palette of green, white, and orange strips.

In the oppressive heat, George Martinez reported to and from fire calls at the Tahitian Village fire station. At his house it was too hot for grilling on the back patio. Even the patio umbrella could not protect from the fierce heat. The sun baked the houses on the cliff top of Tahitian Village as well as the steep drives that led up to them. The houses overlooked the Colorado River, which was evaporating under the sun. The river level lowered steadily.

All over Bastrop, in every house and every shed, on every street and every highway, between every brick and every stone, it was alarmingly hot and dry.

5

THE STRONG WIND

One Sunday in September, a strong wind began to blow. It blew over Bastrop County from north to south. It blew against the dried oak trees and the hot pines, sticky with heated rosin. It blew against the electric lines and poles. The electricity in Bastrop stayed on, but in neighboring cities, power outages were reported even in the early morning.

It was Sunday, September 4, 2011, the day of the annual family-day picnic for the Bastrop Fire Department at Lake Bastrop. The firefighters' tradition in years past had been to grill hamburgers and hot dogs in the red-raftered pavilion open to the lakefront. But this year, due to the burn ban, they wouldn't be grilling.

The wind blew against the twisted oak trees lining the gray park drive leading to Lake Bastrop. It blew Lake Bastrop into a choppy rhythm of white caps, where the firefighters were taking fire boats on test runs and giving rides to children. It wrestled with the volleyball game the older children were playing in the sand along the lake. It snatched napkins from the dinner plates as people helped themselves to the deli sandwiches that had been substituted for the traditional fare.

Two district chiefs walked down to the edge of the water and sat on a bench. They got out their phones and looked at the weather report. Humidity? Almost none. Temperature? High. Wind? Strong. If they doubted their phones, they had only to look at the lake, ruffled in white.

The wind blew on across the lake, buffeting the LCRA power plant and Bluebonnet's power poles and lines. It blew into the alleyways created by the easements around the largest poles, which had been cleared of trees.

Whistling across Highway 21, the wind rattled the metal blades of Mike Gibbons' windmill. It swept around the cows and their long horns in the dry pasture in front of Itsatown. It even knocked over a tree.

Mike Gibbons was not at home the morning of September 4. He was completing a 24-hour canoe race that he, his son, and his daughter-in-law had started the morning before. Although they didn't win, they did canoe the entire 100-mile course.

Mike's wife Shirley came to the end of the race to pick them up. All three were exhausted, having exercised for twenty-four hours instead of sleeping. They felt dozy on the way home.

By the time they got home, the wind was horrendous. Their brows furrowed in concern when they saw the downed tree.

Shirley planned to fly to Albuquerque, New Mexico, to spend a few days with a friend. Even though Mike was weary and the wind was extreme, Mike and Shirley sat on the front porch to chat before her departure. Because of Mike's fatigue, another friend planned to take Shirley to the airport in Austin.

As Mike watched the bending trees, he remembered his firefighting experience. "It would be a really bad day to have a fire," he said.

Mike Gibbons fought fires before he became a paramedic. He knew the difference between a wildfire and a structure fire. Fire trucks cannot get to a wildfire; instead, the fire is fought on foot, with rakes, shovels, or whatever implement is available.

Mike also had experience with wind. In his career as a high-rise welder, he remembered stepping out on the beams of a rising structure when the steel was shiny with ice and the wind was blowing. During his time as a high-rise welder, five people died on the job. One just stepped off the elevator, slipped, and never regained his footing. Although Mike enjoyed the thrill of seeing the world from a unique perspective, it was an unnerving job. As he worked, he learned to have a healthy respect for wind.

The wind sent Debra's pickle swing flying, as if it had an invisible rider. At the little white church building across the road, the wind twisted the movable letters on the sign in front of the church.

Debra was responsible to change the message on the sign, and this week she had posted a verse on each side. One side said, "The Lord is our shield and our defender." The other side said, "He is present in our time of need."

Across the road, the wind buffeted the parsonage where Dean and Debra's pastor lived with his inspiring wife. During the past year, the pastor had felt the need to prepare their church for a disaster, just in case. He started a pantry in the church building to stockpile food. If a disaster hit, it would be helpful to have extra provisions.

Opponents of the disaster program thought the stockpile was selfish. However, the pastor felt that having staples on hand would be an opportunity to share with others if the need ever arose. On the shelves of the pantry, the church members stacked flour, rice, sugar, canned chili, and beans. They stored meat in a freezer. The church family rotated the food, using it for fellowship meals and replacing it with a fresh supply. In addition, if a needy family came to church, the congregation gave them a box of food.

The pastor also encouraged his church members to take measures against forest fires. Most Texans thought of California as the place where forest fires happened, but the pastor knew that forest fires could also happen in Bastrop. As the drought continued, he became more convinced that precautions were in order. He suggested to each member that they prepare a grab bag. Important papers, medications, and a change of clothes could be grabbed at a moment's notice.

He encouraged the people to install or maintain outdoor faucets to which a garden hose could be attached. He asked them to keep their roofs and gutters clear of pine needles and leaves and their lawns free of brush.

On September 4, Debra slept later than usual and awoke from a dream in which she had been walking through a dark woods. A beam of light shone on the path for her next step, but only for one step at a time. Eventually she arrived at a clearing, and the darkness turned to duskiness. She saw a side view of Bastrop Christian Outreach Center, the large church on the other side of Bastrop where she taught homeschooled students at the One Day Academy. She went inside and found long tables loaded with food. She looked outside again and found the nearby field full of tents.

Despite the odd dream, she felt peaceful when she woke up.

The wind blew against Wesley Peschke's bottle house. Margaret's favorite oak tree outside her kitchen window danced and twirled. It rattled the miniature red tricycle gracing the front doorstep.

Always full of foresight, Margaret had been thinking all week about the dry conditions. What would she take with her if there were a fire? She already had a fireproof box with important papers. She placed this box by the front door so they could take it with them if they needed to leave in a hurry.

She walked through the house, noting the things she valued. In one bedroom sat a 160-year-old spinning wheel and a wooden ironing board. A cuckoo clock from Germany resided prominently on the wall. Wesley had kept mementos from his job at Southwestern Bell Telephone Company, such as the blue operator stools he had transformed into kitchen stools. Other items of Wesley's handiwork dotted their house, such as the lamp he had made with a running electric meter and the piece of art he had painstakingly created with Indian corn kernels and butter beans, standing each kernel on end until the glue hardened. Margaret smiled at the cedar chest Wesley had given her the Christmas before their marriage.

Would I take this? Would I take that? she wondered. These things symbolized important times in their lives.

The wind ruffled the hair of Adam and Cindy, who were hosting their son and his family before they moved to Germany. It tossed the pine trees surrounding their house.

Inside, Adam was giving his grandchildren rides on his back. Their son and daughter-in-law were helping with dishes and fixing a bed. Cindy was experiencing back pain and trying to take it easy.

The wind blew against the brick house where Nicholas Cowey and his wife lived. It whistled through their dog Ranger's miniature log cabin. As they headed out to church the morning of September 4, they expected not to be back until evening, since they had afternoon plans.

Working at McKinney Roughs Nature Park, Nicholas knew the heat and drought predisposed Bastrop to fire danger. He felt good about their house, though. It did have a wooden deck and was lined with a few bushes, but it was made of brick. The only way fire could reach it would be through the eaves.

Still, Nicholas had thought of purchasing a fireproof box or renting a safe deposit box at the bank. But what good would those securities do to protect four thousand books, a cabinet of valuable arrowheads, or an antique gun from the French and Indian War?

The wind blew against Bill and Patsy's 370 trees. Inside the once-pink house, Patsy was taking her afternoon nap. Bill was dozing on a recliner in the living room.

Patsy felt uneasy that Sunday, though she didn't know why. She was not afraid of fire. She knew about the wildfires in the middle of nowhere in Texas, but she rarely heard of people needing to evacuate their homes.

The wind moved through the tall pines of Bastrop State Park, swirling around the 75-year-old stone cabins where campers still spent the night. The state park superintendent stepped outside to watch the weather and frowned. If only the day could go by with no trouble, surely the wind would die. If only no trees would fall and no one would rebelliously start a campfire, perhaps things would be okay. He couldn't wait for the day to end.[1]

The wind bounced Mike Fisher's vehicle as he headed out of town to help with power outages in other areas of Bastrop County. Mike Fisher was the man who had coined the term *fire plain* to describe areas like Bastrop where houses and forest come together.

In the neighboring town of Elgin, the power was out. Street lights were not working. Cell phones were not recharging. Air conditioners and freezers grew warm. People on oxygen machines switched to portable tanks and hoped the power would return soon.

Mike Fisher arrived on the scene to help them.

The wind blew over Maxine's on Main, blowing customers in and out the front door with a slam. It rattled the rusty tin roofs of Tommy Hoover's restored village along the Colorado River. It picked trash and tin cans out of dumpsters and sent them rattling. It snatched notices off glass shop doors and sent them sailing. It advertised colored newsprint fliers of previous weeks, rushing them down the streets where they would be trampled.

It blew south over Highway 71 and over Larry Miller's pasture of specialty goats. It lifted their floppy brown ears and whisked away their bleating. Far away, a sister wind buffeted the train on which Larry was working, miles from Bastrop.

It blew down Tahitian Drive and over the brick Tahitian Village Market. It blew shut the car doors of people jumping out to buy gas. It tugged at the removable numbers that advertised the price of gas. Beside the apartment where Ryan was sleeping late, the wind rocked Betsy, the red minivan. Ryan wasn't feeling well, and since he didn't have to work until three, he stayed in bed.

Ryan wasn't expecting a fire, although the thought entered his mind that if there would be a fire, it would be a disaster. However, on September 4, as he tossed in bed, he had an odd feeling that he was missing out on something.

In Tahitian Village, George Martinez and his wife were planning to have family over, since it was a holiday weekend. George had concluded that grilling on his huge concrete patio would be safe, and his wife had prepared the meat.

He had the lighter in his hand and was standing near the patio furniture when a gust of wind rushed past him and snatched up the large patio umbrella. It rose twenty-five feet into the air, like a parachute going the wrong way.

George put the lighter away. The wind was too risky; plans would need to change. "Put the meat away. I'm going over to Benny's Bar-B-Que," he said. His wife knew that he would come back from Benny's with brisket and sausage.

Being a firefighter, George was aware of the fire danger and even held practice sessions with his wife. He would come home from fire calls and say, "Honey, you've got ten minutes to leave. What are you taking with you?"

George taught his wife the back routes out of Tahitian Village. He did not want her to fight traffic out Tahitian Drive with twelve hundred other homeowners.

"Honey, whenever this happens, I'm not going to be here to help you," he would tell her. If there was a bad fire, George would be with the firefighters.

6

THE TREE THAT SNAPPED

Numerous trees fell throughout Bastrop County on the morning of September 4. Some were dead trees. Some were trees weakened by the severe drought. But all the trees landed safely that morning, hidden in the forest, startling only the animals that lived in or around them.

Then, about 2:00 p.m., up in the Circle D subdivision at the edge of the forest, in the wildland-urban interface where the Bastrop houses and Bluebonnet's power poles and the Lost Pines all came together, another tree snapped. After standing through years of Texas drought and wind and rain and cold and heat, through the ninety days of 100-degree weather that summer, through the morning's powerful wind—its branches strained until the tree could hold out no longer. Its trunk broke.

Even if a photographer had been standing close by, he would not have been able to catch the action. Snapped by a gust of incredible wind, the trunk tilted forward. Heartwood splintered. An aroma of freshly cut wood oozed into the wind. The upper branches twirled, grabbing for Bluebonnet's electric wires.

For a fateful moment, the dried leaves and parched twigs grappled with the live wires, wrapping around each other. Then the wires stretched taut. Finally, they too lost the fight and snapped. The loose ends of wire tangled with the tree, and they fell together to the brown grass below. The broken lines began to spark—small sparks hard to see in the daylight.

Had the forest been cool and wet, the sparks would not have produced enough heat to catch hold of the fuel. Had the sparks landed on a cement sidewalk, they would have found no fuel. Had someone been there to step on the sparks or smother them with a fire extinguisher, they would have been deprived of oxygen, and they would have gone out.

Instead, it was hot, there was plenty of dry fuel, and no one stood by to intervene.

THE FIRE TRIANGLE

Fire needs just three things to survive: fuel, oxygen, and heat. Without these three things, a fire will die. A candle flame exemplifies this.

The candle wax is its fuel, liquefying, migrating up the wick, and turning into a flammable gas. If the wax runs out, the flame dies.

The air surrounding the candle contains oxygen. One teaspoon of air contains 400,000 trillion molecules of various gases, mostly nitrogen and oxygen.[1] If a jar is placed over the candle, the flame eats up the oxygen inside the jar and then dies.

The atmosphere in which we normally burn candles contains heat. The colder the environment, the harder it is to maintain a fire. Conversely, a fire will start more quickly the hotter fuel becomes.

THE LOST PINES: GIANT CANDLES

Everything that is alive or was once alive contains carbon. All of these living or once-living things are fuels. Even coal comes from plants long packed together beneath the surface of the earth.

Fires burn fuel just like people's bodies burn calories. Fires burn fuel quickly, and the human body burns its fuel more slowly, but the process is similar. For fires, it is called *combustion*. For people it is called *metabolism*. Engines are the same. They also need oxygen and fuel and heat to run.

Pilot heat is needed to start fires. In the case of a candle, the pilot heat is usually a match. As the pilot heat nears the wick, some of the wax melts and evaporates into the air, like boiling water turning into a cloud of steam. The small "cloud" of gas catches fire, sometimes with a small burst, and a neat flame grows. The hotter the candle is to begin with, the less energy is needed to melt the wax and create the cloud of gas.

The Lost Pines of Bastrop, the loblolly forests, stood like giant candles on Labor Day weekend, ready to burst into flame with the help of the smallest pilot heat. Once heated above 140 degrees by the sun or by a fire, the rosin in the pine trees would turn into extremely flammable vapor.

Although focused on power outages, Mike Fisher was aware of the fire danger. On his way back from Elgin, around 2:00 p.m., he called his staff and told them to open the Emergency Operations Center. No, there had been no known sparks, but the weather conditions felt as unpredictable as the wind whipping the flags on Bastrop's flagpoles.

About the same time, Bastrop's head fire chief, Henry Perry, who was not at the family-day picnic by Lake Bastrop, called one of the district chiefs who had been sitting on the bench watching the weather. He told the district chief to get the boats off the lake and pack up. Without delay, they began following orders.

There had been no fire report, no smoke sighted, and no visible trouble. However, Chief Perry heard that there were thousand-acre fires all over Texas. Ominous fires had popped up in almost every county surrounding Bastrop. This meant that it could only too easily happen in Bastrop County as well. Worse, if it did happen in Bastrop County, the Bastrop Fire Department would be alone. There would be no one to call upon for mutual aid because all the other departments were busy. Even the inmate fire brigade at the nearby prison had been called out to help another county.

> ### UNAVAILABLE BACKUP
> The inmates were only allowed to join the fire brigade if they met certain criteria. They were not allowed to fight in fires that required air packs, the devices that help firefighters breathe, but they could help clean up after such fires.
>
> Because of the high fire danger, the National Forest Service pre-positioned aircraft throughout the drought-baked state of Texas. The closest one to Bastrop was about ninety miles away. But if the surrounding counties were already using these backup assistants, they would not be available when Bastrop needed them.

George Martinez had purchased the brisket and sausage from Benny's and was heading home when he got a text. It was from District Chief Josh Gill. Josh's text emphasized Chief Perry's concern. It informed his fellow firefighters that, just in case they hadn't heard, the surrounding counties had all been called out to fires of their own. If Bastrop had a fire call, they would be on their own.

It was 2:19 p.m.

At almost the same second, a woman living in Circle D on Charolais Drive looked out her window and spotted the beginnings of an inferno. She called 9-1-1 immediately.

The dispatcher who picked up the phone back in Bastrop at 2:20 was sitting in a small, windowless room. The day had started like any other. The dispatchers knew that Mike Fisher was out of town taking care of power outages, but they could not even see how windy it was from their room. They knew about the high fire danger, but that was nothing new.

The caller said, "Fire, please, we have a line down—electric line—and there's a fire."

In the short conversation that followed, it was obvious to the dispatcher that the caller was standing by a window, watching the fire grow as she spoke. By the end of the conversation, the woman began to panic. She said she had to get her children and hung up.[2]

At 2:21, just two minutes after the warning from Josh Gill and just twenty-nine seconds after the woman called, the dispatcher sent out the fire tone to the firefighters of Bastrop County. The musical, metallic tone rang out on the pagers of all the Bastrop firefighters. They all grew quiet, listening.

Josh Gill, who had just finished sending the warning text, heard the tone. It wasn't a surprise, but a shock of adrenaline hit him anyway. It was going to be a busy afternoon.

Alan Donaldson, at home in his house of books and Asian souvenirs, heard the tone. He left his house immediately and drove toward the station. He drove past the fire on his way to the station. Under the sixty-foot pine trees, he could see the flames, still low in the grass, branches, and small trees.

George Martinez, driving home from Benny's with the brisket, heard the tone. He called his wife. "Honey, this is the big one; meet me at the station," he told his wife on the phone. She met him and took the newly purchased meat. One look at his face told her that he was serious.

"Go home and get ready," he told her. "I'll call you when it's time to leave."

Mike Fisher, driving back from the power outages in Elgin, heard the tone. He decided to swing by the fires on his way back.

Back in the dispatch office, the calm Sunday afternoon had vaporized as quickly as the rosin in the pine trees. The normally calm and controlled dispatch office turned into a frenzy. The first call was followed within the next few minutes by ten more calls. With each call received, the dispatchers tracked the fire, recording the location from that particular caller. In this way, they could update the next people who called and the officers on duty.

After the tenth call, Mike Fisher instructed one of the two dispatchers to call in a third co-worker to help them. At first when he said this, the dispatcher was skeptical, thinking she and her partner could handle things. But suddenly there was a flood of calls.

Josh Gill was the first to arrive on scene, just three minutes after the fire call. From where he parked, he could not see the fire. But when he jumped out of his truck, he heard the roar.

When Josh got to where he could see what sounded like a freight train, he was electrified. What had been a fire on the forest floor only minutes before was now torching the tallest trees. As he watched, a sixty-foot loblolly pine tree burst into flame in one motion. The wind carried the heat from the burning tree into the next part of the forest, preheating the rosin in the groups of trees ahead. Flame followed the heat, and the cluster of massive pines roared into flame.

It was already a crown fire. The fire moved through the crowns of the trees as if they were small shrubs.

As the giant trees of the Lost Pines burst into flame, they exploded into pieces. Burning pine cones, chunks of bark, and small twigs whirled into the air, caught the wind, and fell ahead of and to the sides of the fire. Some of these small embers went out before they hit the ground, but others did not.

The burning embers that landed on the ground started the grass around them on fire, then the bushes, then the loose branches. The wind pushed the little fires forward, and they licked up bigger fuel.

When Josh's eyes turned from the eighty-foot flames blasting through the forest, he saw little spot fires jumping up everywhere. With the train-like roar in his ears combined with the rushing wind, Josh reported to dispatch. "I got heavy, heavy fire. . . . It's headed toward county road. It is in the trees."

The welcome wail of sirens broke into the sound of the roaring. Other firefighters and deputies arrived quickly. They leaped into action, firefighters pulling out hoses and deputies stomping on small spot fires, fire extinguishers in hand.

Josh, the incident commander, ordered the others to protect the houses. They pulled trucks up to the structures and leaped out with hoses. They soaked the roofs and walls and directed their hoses toward leaping spot fires.

At 2:33 p.m., after only ten minutes, the firefighters were already exhausted and dripping with sweat. They were losing ground, not gaining it.

"I'm gonna need some more help, Chief," Josh radioed. "Round up the rest of the county and get 'em out here."

"All right, we'll get the resources we can," Chief Perry replied, "uh . . . for you, Josh."

The "uh" communicated much more than the words the chief spoke. Chief Perry knew there was no one to help. There was no one extra to call in. Everyone else was busy fighting their own fires. "The resources we can" was a hopeful phrase, but Chief Perry knew there were no resources within immediate reach.

It was the worst moment of his career, hearing Josh ask for help and knowing there was none.

After radioing the chief, Josh instructed the deputies on scene to stop fighting the fire and start evacuating the people in the houses.

The firefighters were spread throughout the neighborhood. Josh helped trucks set up around several houses. He recognized a house that they had saved recently from a roof fire. Could they save it again?

Another district chief was down the road from Josh, spraying water on the spot fires on the edge of the road and in the forest. Burning embers continued to fall from the sky into the groups of rushing men.

At 2:37 the radio crackled again, for the benefit of anyone who was not on scene: "We got a monster with spot fires everywhere!"

At 2:39 Josh took a moment to evaluate their situation. The main fire was rushing headlong through the forest of houses, through the wildland-urban interface full of people and trees, through the land that Mike Fisher had called a fire plain.

Firefighters were everywhere, hoses circling through the forest floor and around the houses. It was what they were trained to do, but Josh had known almost from the beginning that it was hopeless. The roaring fire was too big. The small fires were too many. In the time it took to extinguish one spot fire, more burning embers had dropped from the sky.

Most of all, there were too many people living in the forest who needed to get out. This was not a time to worry about houses. Deputies began running, knocking on doors, and telling people to get out.

"You are going to have to find me some help," Josh radioed to the Emergency Operations Center. "Things are looking bad out here."

"We are trying to get you aircraft and anything else," was the reply.

"I'm being overrun. This is going to be another Wilderness Ridge Fire," Josh added, just to make sure he'd made his point clear.

PROPHETIC WORDS

If Josh could have picked up the September 15, 2011, edition of the *Bastrop Advertiser*, he would have found this quote on the fifth page: ". . . the fire, whipped by a vengeful wind, made its way across the Lost Pines. It made the Wilderness Ridge Fire look like a birthday candle."[3]

For twenty more minutes, the firefighters fought the losing battle. The radio traffic began to get even more tense.

"I have a wall of fire coming down Charolais."

"Fire is now at Hereford and Cattlemens. I don't know if I can get out of here."

"It sounds like a freight coming. We are having to abandon this house at 154 Charolais. We are not getting anyone killed in this fire. Nobody is getting killed. Need to start a reverse 9-1-1." The reverse 9-1-1 would send an automated evacuation message to every house in the area.

Then something new came—blinding smoke oozing in from all directions. The smoke was deep and dark. As it settled across the forest like a blanket, it hid the dangerous pockets and pillars of orange flame.

Finally, at 3:02 p.m., Josh made the call.

"I want all units off of Charolais. It's blowing up. Use extreme caution. Visibility is zero. Everyone needs to pull out. Come on, come on before you get burned over."

Over the radio, Josh told the firefighters to leave the scene and meet at a motel down the road. It would be a safe place to meet because it had plenty of defensible space: a big, empty lot free of trees.

> ### DEFENSIBLE SPACE
>
> Firefighters, especially those in wildfire-prone areas, have long touted defensible space concepts to homeowners. Having defensible space around a home means that there is as little fuel as possible around the house. Experts encourage landscapers to break shrubs and decorative plants into groups rather than setting them in a continuous line. Grass-like plants and plants with needles are less likely to catch fire than dense plants with broad, dry leaves. Flammable outdoor furniture should be positioned away from the house.
>
> Worst of all, the firefighters report, are wooden attachments to the house, like fences or decks. The fires can easily travel down a fence or across a deck and set the house on fire.
>
> "Keep your defensible space lean, clean, and green," says Rich Gray of the Texas Forest Service.

"Disconnect the hose, let's go, throw it on the ground, let it burn!" yelled a district chief. The firefighters dropped their hoses and ran toward their trucks. The smoke was so thick they couldn't breathe.

Because they couldn't see, they had to yell to let each other know where they were. They could barely hear each other above the roar of the fire and wind. At moments when the wind cleared the air of smoke, huge columns of orange rose like tentacles much too close, grabbing for more fuel.

Most of the people who lived in the forest had already escaped, but some were still there. When they saw the firefighters leave, they became angry. They did not want the firefighters to leave their houses and their pets to burn. They cursed the firefighters and called them cowards.

"My backyard—my house is on fire!" a man screamed.

"Go!" the firefighters yelled back through the smoke.

"Lady, there's nothing I can do for you," a firefighter replied to someone else.

Josh knew the people didn't understand. They were angry and upset because they weren't thinking straight and hadn't stopped to do the math. They didn't realize that Josh could not leave three fire trucks around one house when there were six thousand people who needed to leave the forest immediately.[4] People taking Sunday afternoon naps would never hear their phones ringing. Some people lived so tightly under their trees that they would never see the cloud until it was in their backyard.

The firefighters did not have enough time to fight individual structure fires, nor did they have time to argue with people who refused to evacuate. The more people stayed, the more the firefighters had to worry about them, and the longer it would be before they could start fighting the fire again.

If Josh had tried to protect the area houses with Bastrop fire trucks, there would have been one truck for every sixty-six houses—clearly not enough trucks or firefighters to keep individual houses protected. In fact, had there been more firefighters on hand immediately, it's likely that more lives would have been lost. Because the situation was completely unmanageable, lives were spared by pulling out and fighting the fire at large.

The fire trucks were separated into groups. Once everyone was in a truck, each group got into a line. Josh was at the head of the line in his group. He could not see where he was going; in the smoke, the road wasn't visible. He radioed to the people behind him to stay close. It didn't matter if they rear-ended each other.

Josh drove. When he felt the truck dropping off the side of the road, he turned the wheel slightly to keep the caravan on the road. When he felt the wheels slipping off the other side, he turned the wheel the other way. The heavy-duty trucks clung together in tight lines.

Above the lines of trucks, an orange glow hung over the forest. Even inside the cabs, the firefighters could feel the heat from the fire. Plastic melted on the tops of the trucks.

George Martinez was driving a truck too, with several trucks behind him. The radios cackled with traffic. "Get out! Get out!"

For a moment, he realized that he might die. *I know where my salvation is,* George realized, thinking of his faith in Christ. But there was little time to think about dying. He couldn't see clearly where he was driving, and he had to focus on leading the others out.

Alan Donaldson was in another area of the fire with a crew of five trucks when the blanket of smoke descended. In the thick gray, Alan realized he didn't know from which direction the fire was coming. Or were there many fires? They could not see. What if they drove their five trucks down the wrong road, straight into the fire?

One of the five trucks was parked in a yard. A young firefighter jumped in to drive it onto the road so they could leave. Suddenly the area between Alan and the young man burst into a wall of flame.

He's gone! Alan thought. *We lost a man!*

Then the truck, with the young man driving it, burst through the wall of flame. The fire truck did not catch fire or explode. The five trucks were together again. But they were still trapped, and they did not know which way to go.

Alan knew there was no one to help them. Still, he wanted the others to know where they were. Even if they were trapped and burned, at least the other firefighters would know where their journey had ended.

"Mayday, Tender 233, we've got five trucks trapped on Charolais Drive," Alan radioed.

Like the other lines of trucks, they followed each other bumper to bumper, completely blind. They did not know if they were going the right way. They could feel the heat from the fire through the walls of the trucks, and they wondered if the trucks would explode.

Then, suddenly, the smoke cleared and revealed a beautiful azure sky. They could see, and they were safe. With relief, the drivers headed out of the area as fast as they could. There was still an apocalypse in the rearview mirrors. Many long hours extended ahead of them. But for the moment, under the wide, blue Texan sky, all was well. They were alive.

7

THE RUNAWAY SCRAPE OF 2011

Mike Fisher detoured close to the fire on his way back to Bastrop. Before he got there, he saw a cloud of smoke pluming up into the air, higher and higher.

Mike, well-versed in fire science, knew it was a convective column. He knew it would rise at least ten to twelve thousand feet into the air until it cooled down to the temperature of the air around it. He knew the smoke would drift hundreds of miles away, out over the Gulf of Mexico.

When he got closer, Mike saw the wind whipping the fire through the grass and trees like a giant combine, hungry for more. Driven by the wind, the fire would follow the fuel, of which there was plenty in drought-baked Bastrop. Mike knew that the fire would breathe out burning embers ahead of itself, making it impossible to surround with trucks or hoses.

As he drove through the fire plain, between the trees and the houses, there was one thing he did not know. *Will the people leave in time?* Mike wondered. *Will they be smart enough to leave?* He had a hunch that the people living in these rural areas under the pines and the blue sky would be able to do it. He suspected that they were more resourceful than people living in the cities. But he still felt apprehension.

> ## THE RUNAWAY SCRAPE OF 1836
>
> When Texas got tired of being part of Mexico, their War for Independence occurred. In Bastrop, the fighting was at first just a far-off rumor that was easy to ignore. Sometimes soldiers passed through Bastrop on their way south to fight the Mexicans, as Davy Crockett of Tennessee did as he headed for the Alamo in San Antonio.
>
> When word reached Bastrop that the Alamo had been captured, however, the war became much more real. Panic set in all over Texas. People began to flee to escape the Mexican Army, which was marching north in triumph. Unlike September 2011, Bastrop was flooded in 1836. The spring had been exceptionally wet, which made traveling extremely difficult. Besides fearing the army, citizens were endangered by Indians, disease, and cold. When people died, the bodies were abandoned beside the road.
>
> At Trinity River there was a traffic jam of Texans headed for Louisiana. Because of all the rain, the river was extra wide and the ferry ride more difficult. The Bastropians had to wait in line for a week to get ferried across.
>
> In his book *History of Bastrop County, Texas, Before Statehood*, Kenneth Kesselus records that a local woman fleeing the army came from out of town and through Bastrop. The shopkeepers of Bastrop had already fled, but one of them had left his store open. He had left a note on the door inviting anyone to help themselves to anything they needed; they could pay him if they ever returned. The woman selected a pair of boots, which proved invaluable through the many miles of mud.[1]

One hundred seventy-five years after the Runaway Scrape of 1836, Bastrop was evacuating again with haste and uncertainty, some leaving their homes for the last time. The Indians and soldiers of the past had been replaced by a force of nature that could not be surrounded, reckoned with, or predicted.

The Bastrop County deputies had experience evacuating people, but nothing on this scale. "As I looked down the road, I saw a wall of fire," one of the first deputies on scene said. He realized that the fire was not going to stop.[2]

The deputies watched empty vehicles burst into flame, their owners fleeing on foot to catch a ride with someone else.

The cars that escaped rushed down the road, smoke swirling around them. Fire rose in the grass on both sides of the road, reaching out long fingers of flame in the wind.

"Y'all need to get out!" the deputies yelled to everyone they could find. Some deputies circled through neighborhoods with loudspeakers and sirens, trying to make enough noise so that everyone could hear and be warned.

Hurried shouts volleyed between rescuers.

"Is anybody in here?"

"I don't know—I checked the house down there; you might want to check it again."

"Is Charolais Drive clear?"

"Yes!"

One officer drove through an area that had been declared clear of people and saw a man on his roof. "What are you doing?" he hollered at the man.

The man explained that the house he was standing on was his mother's only possession, and he would not leave it under any conditions, even though he did not have a hose with which to fight the fire.

The officer finally realized that the man would not be persuaded, and he left the scene. He couldn't stop thinking about the man, but he never knew the end of the story. Had the fire scared the man enough to get off the roof? Had he realized that his life was more important than a house?

A healthcare worker was at home alone, totally unaware of the fire, when a deputy pounded on his door.

"Grab your keys; the fire is here," the deputy said.

The healthcare worker snapped to attention, but he was skeptical. *I'm from the country,* he thought. *These city officials get all worked up over nothing. When they say it's close, they probably mean half a mile away yet.*

The disbelief was evident in his eyes.

"You don't understand," the deputy said. "You and I have to leave *now*. We may have time to save ourselves."

The man got in his vehicle and followed the deputy out. Smoke poured across the hood of his car. Fire rose on both sides of the road, flashing from tree to tree. Fire fell from the sky, burning pine cones and branches that started new fires.

The fire never stayed in the same place. It arched over the entire road, curling, dancing, and changing in the wind. One moment a tree stood beside the road. The next moment it was a pillar of fire.

Finally the deputy and the healthcare worker could go no farther. In the glow of dancing flames and the fog of smoke, they turned around, questions screaming in their minds. Would there be another way out? Would they find the way out before the flames crept into their vehicles? Would the smoke overtake them with blindness? Would they suffocate from lack of oxygen? There were many ways to die, but the only way to survive was through escape.

The next road they chose was better. They made it out between walls of fire.

When the healthcare worker realized he was alive and safe, he called his neighbors. Thankfully, they were in San Antonio that day.

His skepticism had long since vanished. He told his neighbors, "The only thing I can tell you is that your house is on fire. All of Bastrop County is on fire."

8

ESCAPEES

Before the deputies came knocking, Debra Pahlow heard about the fire from a friend.

It was early afternoon when they got the call that said there was a fire and they would likely have to evacuate.

Debra's boys joined the evacuation effort. They walked down Alum Creek Drive to their near neighbors, knocking on doors and sharing the message.

In this neighborhood, a spirit of adventure was in the air. No one could see smoke or smell burning pine wood. The fire was off on Charolais Drive. No one expected it would reach them, but it was fun to play evacuation.

Everyone in the family began packing. Debra, an educator at heart, reminded them to take their school books. Jorja, Debra's seven-year-old daughter, carefully collected everything she needed.

Jorja had been born in the house. Debra thought of her birth, the sense of peace that washed over her right before the baby was born as she repeated a memorized Scripture over and over to herself. "Fear thou not; for I am with thee: be not dismayed . . ." When the baby's color wasn't quite right because she had swallowed too much meconium, the midwife and other helpers were worried. They watched the baby closely to decide whether she would have to be taken to the hospital. Only Debra was not worried. The sense of peace was so strong, she knew the baby would be okay. After thirty minutes, the crisis was over and little Jorja was fine.

Now Jorja was a little lady with great foresight. When she packed, she packed right. She even packed her future curtains, the ones she meant to use after her parents remodeled her room.

They packed their aging van and truck full of teacher's supplies, photo albums, and other possessions. However, they wanted to stay together, so they parked those two vehicles at the end of the cul-de-sac and climbed into their station wagon, driving off together.

Debra thought of Hurricane Rita a few years before. Before the mighty storm made landfall in East Texas, the Bastrop area had been warned about the potential of winds reaching seventy miles per hour. The Pahlows had gone to Holly's house and held a hurricane party. Holly's house was not much safer, since it was also a mobile home—but fewer trees surrounded it.

Debra had committed their house to the Lord at that time. She knew God had built the house anyway. "Lord, if you need to take the house, it's okay. But if you do, just give me the grace not to fall apart, and to be a good witness until it's all said and done." This had been Debra's prayer.

The house was spared from Hurricane Rita. Now, on the fourth of September 2011, the prayer fit again. Across the road at the small white church, the verses Debra posted were still on the sign: "The Lord is our shield and our defender" and "He is present in our time of need."

The Pahlows' pastor and wife got a call from friends about the fire. They were not at home, but they quickly drove toward the white church. Already, the northern sky was black with smoke.

"This is a bad one!" the pastor kept saying as he took in the scene.

As they neared their church and parsonage, they also drew closer to the zone of action. Pulling past the trees, they were suddenly able to look down a road leading into the mayhem.

"It looked like a horror movie," the pastor's wife recalled. "Pitch black smoke, people running, fire vehicles, policemen, emergency lights."

They couldn't see any flames at that point, but they could smell the smoke. As they pulled up to the church, they discovered several people had already retreated there to find safety. As the pastor opened the church to let them in and turned on the church air conditioning, his wife drove her scooter up the ramp into their house and began packing important items. As she packed, she was thinking she would be gone for maybe three hours. She gathered about four bags and her husband's computer.

When the pastor saw a deputy nearby, he went over and informed him that the church was open and had air conditioning and water.

"What are you doing here?" the deputy asked. "You're supposed to be evacuated."

The pastor looked down the easement cut around the large power poles. Looking down this long tunnel between the trees, he could now see flames.

The pastor and his wife packed their vehicle, after which the pastor motioned to his wife to drive away.

"I'm going to stay and try to save everything," he said resolutely. Besides the church and the parsonage, he wanted to protect his exterior office building and the cabin/woodworking shop normally occupied by his elderly uncle. The uncle was receiving care in a nursing home, but his things were still there, including the wooden bowls and candlesticks he had carved in the wood shop.

But his wife was resolute too. "I'm not leaving unless you leave," she said. Leave her husband to escape a forest fire after fifty years of marriage? She was not interested.

In the end they left together. As they were leaving, they saw flames in the path that was cleared around the large power poles. However, they were sure the four-lane highway would stop the fire from going any farther.

They drove to a relative's home in Austin and spent the night there, with no idea what was going on at home. The pastor made an effort to contact church members, including Dean and Debra Pahlow, and eventually accounted for most of them.

After his wife left for the airport, Mike Gibbons prepared himself for a long sleep. His son and daughter-in-law, who lived next door, were already sound asleep.

Mike Gibbons benefited by his wife's departure. Had it not been that Shirley was about to leave, Mike would have gone to bed instantly when he got home instead of staying up to talk on the porch. He would have likely fallen into a deep sleep, his muscles aching from the 24-hour canoe trip. He may not have awakened to any phone calls or pounding on the door.

As it was, Mike was the first of the three to realize there was a fire. After he got a phone call from his mother informing him about the threat, he tried to call his son and daughter-in-law. Deciding they must be sleeping so deeply they would not answer their phones, he ran to their house and pounded on the door, finally waking them up. After that, Mike took his mother to a community center where evacuees gathered. His son and daughter-in-law went with them.

Meanwhile, on the way to Albuquerque, Shirley's flight connected in El Paso. Upon landing in El Paso, a flight attendant ran to the front of the plane. She had bad news for the captain: his house was burning. Shirley, sitting near the front of the plane, heard the word "Bastrop."

Both the captain and Shirley wanted to go home immediately. Inside the airport, they tried as hard as they could to rearrange their schedules. The flight to Albuquerque was delayed for forty-five minutes in an effort to work with them. In the end, it couldn't be done. The plane had to go on to Albuquerque, with the captain and Shirley on it.

Shirley was a wreck. She tried calling Mike, but he didn't answer. She tried calling her son. He didn't answer, nor did her daughter-in-law. Finally, she thought of her boss at the *Bastrop Advertiser*. His wife answered her call. Shirley, relieved to hear a familiar voice, hoped to hear that the fire was not as bad as she feared.

But that was not what she heard. Her boss's house was already burning.

On Sunday afternoon Margaret Peschke heard five sirens go past. She knew they hadn't gone far because the noise of the sirens did not disappear into the distance.

Whatever's happening, it's bad and it's close, she thought.

Margaret called the Bastrop dispatcher. Previously, she had written down the dispatcher's number so she would have it on hand for just such a situation.

A dispatcher in the windowless room back in Bastrop managed to answer her call and told her that there was a fire up in Circle D, and the people in that area were evacuating.

Circle D was not far away. "We need to get ready," Margaret told her husband. "The fireproof box is right there by the door."

Wesley and Margaret walked through the house. There was her grandma's trunk. The 160-year-old spinning wheel. The cedar chest Wesley had given her.

Margaret looked at the 21-foot shelves in the living room, loaded with memories. She saw the photos from their dating days and the topper from their wedding cake. Looking at them always reminded Margaret of those warm days in El Paso when she fell in love with Wesley. Wesley had called her arrogant. He had said it was good that it didn't rain much in El Paso, because Margaret had her nose in the air, and she would have drowned. Still, he stayed in El Paso even though he had been planning to leave. And Margaret married him even though she had been planning to be a single missionary.

For a while, they lived in the mountains of California in a cheap duplex with mismatching furniture. While they lived there, Margaret had given birth to surprise twins. Soon after the birth, Margaret had a seizure and would have thrown one of the newborn twins had she not just handed the baby to the nurse.

After the seizure, Margaret was overcome with fear and guilt. She told the nurse that God was probably punishing her for marrying Wesley instead of being a missionary.

"God isn't like that," the nurse had said. And eventually Margaret came to believe the truth of her words. Wesley had a way of making her feel secure. Even when they lived in a run-down house and made do with whatever they had, she had felt safe.

As Margaret looked through the house now, she saw the twins' wedding pictures and her great-grandmother's Amish bonnet. She saw the souvenirs from Honduras, Haiti, and Mexico.

Do I take this? Do I take that? she wondered. She looked at her computer. It would be hard to move. They could take it, but she decided to leave it.

Well, I'll be back in a few days, she assured herself. They took the fireproof box, the gold-leaf Indian picture, and a few family photos.

As they drove away, Margaret looked at the bottle house, where they had eaten so many picnic meals. Sometimes they had eaten three meals a day out there. They could not take the bottle house with them. She looked at her favorite oak tree outside her kitchen window, the one that always reminded her that God was good. She could not take the tree. She saw Wesley's little chicken house with the new chickens just beginning to lay eggs. The chickens would have to stay too.

The deputies knocked on Patty Timmons' metal gate.

"Can I help you?" she called out to them. She was surrounded by tall pines and could see nothing.

"Yes, ma'am, the fire is on you," the deputy replied. "Get out now."

Patty and her husband followed his advice. They jumped into their vehicle. They only had time to grab their dog Shadow. They knew that trying to catch the cats would be time-consuming and possibly unsuccessful. Patty never thought of grabbing her scrapbook with the pictures of her father; there was no time.

They drove to the line where everyone had been told to cross and not come back. It was close to Peach Street, across from Lake Bastrop where the firefighters had been picnicking only hours before. Now they could see the cloud of smoke. As they sat in their vehicle, Patty looked at all the other cars, her neighbors from the Lost Pines. In addition to the worried faces looking nervously out their windows, a cat or a dog peered out of nearly every car.

Adam and Cindy went on a morning outing with their son and daughter-in-law, who were making a last visit before their planned move to Germany. During the picnic, they had all deposited their cell phones into a duffel bag for safekeeping.

After they came home that afternoon, Cindy was handing sheets to her daughter-in-law when she heard a muffled ring. It was her cell phone, still in the duffel bag. She picked it up and said, "Hello."

"Mom, what are you all doing? Don't you know something is going on?" It was her other son, who lived in Bastrop.

"What are you talking about?"

Her son, who was driving, repeated himself. "Something's going on!" His voice sounded hysterical. Cindy was shocked and totally confused. She hadn't noticed anything unusual. None of them had. They knew it was really windy, but the pine trees often bent in strong winds.

"Calm down," she told him.

"People are freaking out on the side of the road!" he said. "There's something in the air." Even though he could see some smoke, her son did not know what was going on. He supposed maybe something had blown up.

Cindy quietly stepped out on the porch, not wanting to alarm anyone. She could smell smoke, but glancing at the sky, she could only see a small triangle of gray between the tree tops.

"You need to leave," her son was saying.

Cindy decided that, before she would alarm the entire family and the children, she would drive just a little way down the road where she could see better. She told Adam what she was doing and then slipped away.

Cindy drove to Terry's Corner, the gas station on the corner of Highway 21 and FM (Farm to Market) 1441. Long before she arrived, she could see the mob of cars at Terry's Corner. Groups of people stood at attention beside the sign advertising diesel for $3.56 a gallon. Some pushed buttons on cell phones or held the phones to their ears. Some stood tensely straight and stiff, while others pointed. A woman stood at a distance with her hand held to her mouth.[1]

Cindy pulled to the side of the road and dialed 9-1-1. She had to know what was going on! But the 9-1-1 office did not answer. The dispatchers in their little room were flooded with calls.

"God, please let them answer the phone!" she prayed. She continued dialing 9-1-1.

Finally a dispatcher answered. "Ma'am, I need to know what's going on," she said to the lady who answered the phone.

"There's a fire. Can you tell me where you live?"

"Cardinal Drive."

"You need to evacuate."

She turned to go back, but fire trucks were blocking her path. She was forced to pull off the road to get around them. Off the road, the wheels of her car caught in the underbrush. She was stuck.

"God, whatever's going on, just guide us through this because I don't know what's going on," she prayed as she frantically dialed Adam's cell phone.

To her dismay, his phone began ringing inside her car.

Neither her son nor daughter-in-law answered either. She realized that their phones were probably still in the bag where she had found hers, where they could not be readily heard.

Finally in desperation, Cindy stepped hard on the gas pedal. The car lurched forward, plowing through underbrush. She rushed home and into the house. Her son was washing dishes, and her daughter-in-law was in the shower. "We need to evacuate," she said without preamble.

Running to the bathroom door, she knocked. "You need to get out!" she hollered to her daughter-in-law.

"Is there really a fire?" they all asked her. For a few minutes, her family couldn't believe she was serious. They hadn't heard any previous warning.

Cindy started grabbing family photos off the wall. That's when her family finally took her seriously. They also began to see the trailers and cars going by on the road. Her son and daughter-in-law grabbed important documents.

Cindy grabbed a few clothes and photo albums. With a few possessions, the adults picked up the children and headed for the vehicles.

Outside, ashes were falling from the sky. Suddenly overwhelmed with emotion, Cindy thought of the big box of family photos she had not grabbed. She paused.

"Mom, hurry up, we gotta go," her son said.

Adam was just rushing out of the house. "Could you please go get the boxes of photos?" she asked her husband.

By now everyone was scared, and they really didn't want to go back, but they did. Cindy went back inside to show them which boxes she wanted. Loaded with boxes, they returned and climbed into the vehicles.

They could feel the heat now. They pulled out onto the road into bumper to bumper traffic. Cindy drove her car, and their dog jumped in with her. Adam drove their truck. Their son and daughter-in-law also drove in separate vehicles. As they drove, Cindy's daughter-in-law called her, overcome with anxiety.

"It's going to be okay," Cindy told her. Somehow, she still couldn't believe that the house would actually burn. She felt confident that the firefighters would be able to get the fire under control soon.

They were not directly following each other, but Cindy understood that her son would be getting gas at Terry's Corner. When she got to Highway 21, she tried to turn toward Terry's Corner, but the police told her that way was blocked. Frantically, she explained that her son and family had just gone that way.

"I'm sorry, ma'am, there's no way you can go that way," the official explained.

As she turned around, Cindy prayed and called one of the others. Sure enough, they had turned away from Terry's Corner as well and were waiting for her. When they were reunited, they decided to find something to eat and try to sit down and relax. They drove eighteen miles north to Elgin and ate pizza with the grandchildren.

Nicholas and his wife were driving away for the afternoon when a friend called them and urgently informed them about the fire. Nicholas turned around immediately. As he drove back to their house, he thought about the years of work it represented. The carefully filed insects and arrowheads. The guns and costumes he had collected and purchased. The four thousand books. He thought about one book in particular that had been valued at $12,000. A very old book from Germany, it was made of copperplate lithography sheets, a precursor to modern printing. The sheets folded out three or four times. Besides that favorite, he thought of his shelf of books on plants and another shelf on animals. He thought of his hymnal collection, his room full of history books, his forty favorite books on Lewis and Clark, and the original peace medals he owned. He thought of his map collection of 250 original lithographs, hand-painted maps from before the time of Lewis and Clark. He thought of the microscopes and telescopes that they had planned to use if they had a chance to homeschool children.

Though Nicholas knew they were not supposed to go back, he tried anyway. He reasoned that even if he could grab his $12,000 book, it would be a worthwhile trip. He knew all the back roads, so even though the main roads were blocked off, Nicholas felt confident he could get back in.

The police knew the back roads too. By the time Nicholas got to them, even these were blocked. The only option would have been to walk. Nicholas decided it wasn't worth the risk.

Later, a neighbor told him it was the right choice.

"Nicholas, you wouldn't have been able to stop this thing; you wouldn't have been able to save your house," the man said. "I saw it heading for your house, and it scared me."

Although Efrain and Debi were very aware of the drought, they never expected a forest fire to come to them. Debi remembered a small fire once before, started by an electric line, but that fire was put out quickly.

On Sunday afternoon, Efrain got a call from a friend who had a police scanner.

"Do you know there's a fire on Charolais?" the friend asked.

"What?" Efrain was surprised. "That's not far away."

He stepped onto the back porch. His eyes moved over the scene in astonishment. The forest was belching smoke and fire, with gray, orange, and black rolling together in the sky. A sound like the buzzing of bees filled the air.

When Debi saw the ominous sight, she immediately called their son, who was with a cousin. "We're gonna lose the house," she informed him abruptly.

"We'll be there in five minutes," the son said.

Debi pulled a vehicle onto the road. It was a second vehicle, and she thought maybe they could come back and get it later.

Efrain went out the back of the house, picked up a garden hose, and began to soak the house. Then his eyes strayed to the sky, where the colors ran together like an abstract painting. He felt so shocked that he could not move. He stood with the garden hose at his side, the water forming a useless pool at his feet. He suddenly realized that soaking the log house was futile. Leaving the hose, he went into the house and tried to catch his breath. Even though he had been watering the house for only about five minutes, he felt exhausted. He went to the metal filing cabinets and began to thumb through the files. What papers were the most important? What should he take?

Then Efrain thought about their elderly neighbor. They knew he always took his medication in the afternoon and fell into a deep sleep. He would never wake up on his own. Efrain ran out of his house and over to the neighbor's metal gate. It was locked.

Several other neighbors ran up as Efrain rattled the gate. The neighbors grouped around the metal gate, their faces white and tense. One of the neighbors, a tiny young woman, offered to run up to the elderly man's house if the others boosted her over the gate.

The group of neighbors lifted her easily, and she clambered down the other side of the gate. "Don't knock! Pound!" Efrain yelled after her as she ran up to the door.

Efrain's son and cousin arrived. They had seen fire very close.

"Mom and Dad, just go," they told Debi and Efrain. "We'll get some stuff for you." Their son also offered to help the elderly neighbor leave. The young woman had managed to wake him and open the gate, but the man was very groggy and not at all convinced that his afternoon nap should be interrupted.

Efrain and Debi drove away with the things they had collected, thinking they might be able to return and help their son. But when they reached Terry's Corner, they realized there would be no going back. Under no circumstances would the officers let anyone back into the danger zone.

People were gathering at the gas station. They sat in their vehicles or stood with their eyes on the sky, ready to escape. Every time something exploded with a *BOOM,* the crowd cringed.

Another neighbor called Ephrain and Debi as they sat at Terry's Corner. "Should I leave?" the neighbor asked.

"Get out!" Efrain hollered into the phone.

Debi saw her son approach in the crowd. "Where is your cousin?" she asked him.

"Oh, I left him at Billy's house," he said.

Billy—the medicated neighbor behind the gate. Debi's ears tingled in disbelief. Her nephew was alone in the fire zone, helping the neighbor get his things.

Debi found a highway patrolman and told him what had happened. She wanted to go get her nephew herself, but the patrolman told her that he would go.

Back at Billy's house, Debi's nephew pleaded with the old man to get up and get moving. The old man slowly got up and began to go through the house, carefully collecting the things he wanted to take with him. The young man ran to the window. The situation outside was getting desperate. He ran back to the old man.

"It's coming!" the young man screamed in the old man's ear. Soon they would be trapped. The highway patrolman Debi had spoken with came up to the house and told the man he must leave immediately. Still the man complained.

"You are leaving now!" Debi's nephew yelled. "Either with me or the patrolman!"

Finally, the old man consented. With fire in the rearview mirror, they escaped to Terry's Corner.

René and Kathy were not at home when the fire started. They were driving toward home when they saw a huge cloud of smoke.

"It looks like it's over our house," René told Kathy.

They called their son, who was at home in his newly remodeled room. With relief they heard him answer the phone. He didn't sound at all alarmed. They asked him to look outside to see if there was any smoke.

"Yes!" he answered after looking. "In the backyard."

"Get dressed," they told him. "We'll be there soon."

René and Kathy made it up their road before it was blocked by officials. They parked and jumped out. They didn't know if they should grab their garden hose and prepare to fight, or if they should collect their valuables and leave. As they deliberated, a sheriff drove up and answered their question. He told them to leave.

They decided to take their RV and put valuables into it. They backed it up to the house, and it promptly got stuck in the soft sand. By the time they got it out, they had lost thirty minutes, and there was no time to gather things. The smoke was swirling closer.

Patsy Ludwig got up early from her nap on this Sunday afternoon. She walked through the living room where her husband was half asleep in his recliner. She walked out to the porch, which faced the forest to the east. About this time, she heard a boom.

Walking out into the yard, she could see the sky. Towering above the 370 trees was a mammoth gray cloud.

Galvanized, she whirled and rushed back into the house. "Bill, get up! Get up right now! I'm not kidding—there's a fire and it's going to be a monster."

Bill jerked around. "How do you know that?"

"Come look," Patsy replied.

Together they hustled down to the end of the porch and looked up at the sky. Now they could almost see the flame, a kind of glow at the bottom of the massive stirring of the black cloud.

"We've got to make every minute count," Patsy said. "We need to get everything that we can't buy. Get all the cages for the dogs. Get Grandpa's paintings." They gathered their computers, the paintings, the stamp and coin collections, and the animals. Patsy grabbed her Bible and a folder with certificates and tax papers.

Thirteen minutes after they saw the cloud, Patsy and Bill drove down their lane. They stopped at the end of the lane before pulling onto the road. Patsy climbed out of the car and hurried across the road to the house of a neighbor man. Patsy worried that he would not be aware of what was going on. She pounded on his door.

"Get out, get out, get out! Fire, fire, fire!" Patsy yelled.

The old man came to the door. "I heard a boom," he said in a daze.

A police officer had pulled up to the end of the driveway. He came over and commanded, "Get in your car and leave NOW. Take nothing with you."

As they drove away from their home, Patsy looked back. She could see flames. The smoky smell of burning wood already bit into their nostrils.

"Oh, please, dear God, bless us," she begged over and over.

When they got close to Home Depot in Bastrop, they parked on the hill and settled in to watch the sky. During the three hours they sat on the hill, they remembered all the essentials they had forgotten. "We left without a single piece of clothing or a toothbrush—nothing practical," Patsy said. They had even forgotten their medications.

Larry Miller was two hundred miles away, close to Houston, working on the trains. His cell phone was hidden away. If he was caught talking on his cell phone, he could be fired and fined $20,000. When the train arrived at the place in the station where employees were allowed to use their phones, Larry retrieved his phone.

He had forty missed calls.

When he saw they were calls from his family, he instantly assumed that his father had had a heart attack. He called his daughter back and found that his father was okay—but Bastrop County was on fire, and the flames were rushing toward his property. Larry's daughter and son-in-law and cousin had collected the few things they could take. They cut the fence to set the goats free, but there was no time to pack up the expensive show goats and take them along.

Two hundred miles away, Larry thought about his fine herd of goats. He thought about the years he had spent collecting the tools in his favorite shed. He thought about his tractors and the prize sailfish he had bagged.

Perhaps it was good that he was not at home, he realized. Could he have stood by and left the property, with all those things? Knowing himself, he was pretty sure he could not have left.

On Sunday afternoon Jimmy Mack had gone outside to add an extra length to his garden hose—not to fight fire, but to water his trees. The power had blinked off, but he concluded that there was an awesome thunderstorm going on somewhere. He could feel the strong wind, but because he lived in the trees, he did not notice the fire coming until a police officer paid him a visit.

"What are you still doing here?" the officer hollered at him.

It wasn't long before Jimmy and his wife could hear the explosions and see trees combusting whole. Still, it took them twenty minutes to leave. One problem was that they were trying to retrieve their favorite cat, the one named Kathmandu after the capital of Nepal. It was hiding under their waterbed and refused to come out.

Finally, when Jimmy was convinced they would have to leave without the cat, he poked a mop under the bed. The cat ran out, and he and his wife caught it by each running down a different side of their kitchen island.

After George Martinez escaped from the Circle D area with the other firefighters, he called his wife. Even though the fire was still far from Tahitian Village, it was moving fast. "It's time to go," he told her. He encouraged her to call all her friends who lived nearby as well.

The Tahitian Village subdivision had an email group to email announcements to everyone in the village, perhaps in the case of a missing dog or a suspicious person or vehicle. Today the email group was used to alert residents that they might need to evacuate soon. However, not everyone would check email that day, so George's wife called her friends. Later, they found out that her calls reached some family members who were separated from each other. The families said her calls saved their lives.

Sounds from the outside world invaded Ryan Terranova's apartment walls. A helicopter flew over, and he heard vehicles passing. There was commotion outside, but he was too sleepy to be concerned.

Finally his mom called from Tahitian Village Market across the street.

"You need to get dressed and come over before you can't cross the road," she said.

Over at the gas station, Ryan climbed out of Betsy, his faithful red minivan, and looked up. It was a horror scene. Gray and orange billowed together in the sky. For a second it would be just an orange glow, and then flames would appear over the tops of the trees. From behind the gas station, the sun still shone from clear skies in the west. To the east, unearthly gloom huddled under the broiling gray-orange sky. The gloom swirled around the Citgo sign in front of the shop, advertising gasoline for $3.49. Ryan smelled gas and rubber.

Tahitian Drive began to choke with traffic, the entire subdivision trying to slip out of the bottleneck at once. Ryan made phone calls to friends who lived nearby, checking to see if they knew they should evacuate. The fire had arrived.

As he watched the road, he saw a tow truck drive up. It was pulling an RV, a trailer, and a boat, all linked together in a train about forty feet long. He saw another vehicle packed to the hilt with children and belongings. Trailing behind were two dogs, leashed to fifteen-foot ropes tied to the back. The vehicle crept along at the side of the road. The dogs jogged along to keep up. The children leaned out the windows, squirting their pets with water bottles to stave off the severe heat. The road was choked.

Ryan saw a motorcycle that could have easily passed the other vehicles. Ryan called to him, suggesting that he go around the larger vehicles. The man replied that he was with family in other vehicles and didn't want to leave them behind.

One of the friends whom Ryan called said that his mother was sleeping late in another house. She had taken her medication and probably wouldn't wake up no matter how loudly someone pounded on the door. Ryan took the friend to her house. Flames were only sixty feet away when they arrived. They rushed inside and found the friend's mother in a deep stupor, but they woke her and helped her away to safety.

9

SAVING LIVES FIRST

After the firefighters regrouped at the motel, they decided to focus on helping people escape until they were certain everyone was out. All afternoon they drove up and down the roads. They knocked on people's doors and shouted at them, "You must leave now! The fire is coming!"

Many people had already left. Others knew there was a fire and were already packing their bags. Some people looked up at the sky in surprise and saw the cloud of smoke behind the trees for the first time.

The cloud of smoke was so big it blocked out parts of the sky. Some parts of the cloud were gray. Other parts were white or black. At the bottom, the cloud glowed orange.

The firefighters spread out. Some of them continued checking houses on Highway 21. They passed the little white church with the sign on which Debra had posted verses portraying God's strength and comfort. Some firefighters went to Tahitian Village, where the residents of the twelve hundred homes were all trying to get out of the same narrow lane at once. Other firefighters drove on down Highway 71.

The fire, which had quickly jumped Highway 21, now jumped

Highway 71. One of the district chiefs drove up a side street and passed Larry Miller's pasture full of goats. On the other side of the road he saw a man with a garden hose. When the district chief told him to leave, the man with the garden hose refused. The district chief asked for his name just in case he didn't make it out.

The district chief stopped to pound on the door of another house. When no one answered, he finally turned to leave. As he turned, a man opened the door. He confessed that he had decided he wasn't going to get up, but he decided that if someone was pounding that hard, he'd better get up to see what was happening.

What was happening was that the fire was jumping the four-lane highway and spreading in every direction. The Highway 71 crew made a few efforts to bat out the embers and wash down the flames from the side of the road, but it was useless. The wind was still gusting, and for every fire they put out, more started. The district chief's fire hat blew off his head and tumbled down the road in the wind. By the time he reached it, the grass around him was on fire. By the time he retrieved the hat and returned to his truck, small flames were licking at the grass beneath the truck. It was time to leave.

REFUSALS TO EVACUATE

Early one morning a frantic woman begged officers to find her husband. He had gone back to their house after the roads were blocked off, and she had not seen him or heard from him since four o'clock the previous afternoon.

The officers sent the woman to a shelter, taking her cell phone number so they could contact her. They drove between barricades and walls of fire to the address the woman had given them. The house was still standing, but the trees around it were burning. The officers ran down the driveway yelling, "Sheriff's office!" They could see a figure inside the house.

The man came out with a wet towel on his head. The

officers ordered him to go with them and told him that his wife had sent them. They found out that he had avoided the barricades by parking in a lot and walking to his house to try to save it. The officers let him borrow a phone to call his wife. He stayed composed on the phone, but when he was reunited with his family, he began to weep.

Some of the officers struggled with the animosity they received during the evacuations. While firefighters and volunteers were praised and thanked on public signs, law enforcement was seldom mentioned.

"I was threatened to be shot, almost hit by a car going through a barricade, cussed at and yelled at by people. There were only thirty officers trying to patrol the entire county to keep these people safe. We were risking our lives to help people, and in return, we were treated so ugly. My home and family needed to be evacuated, and I couldn't deal with that because I was helping other people," one officer said.[1]

WHY EVACUATE?

The evacuation problem is not uncommon in disasters. People believe they can save their house by staying, and they might be right. But at the same time, every fire behaves differently, and risking lives to save houses is simply not worthwhile. What looks like a small grass fire may suddenly jump into the trees, dropping burning embers over a wide area. By refusing to leave, residents risk not only their lives, but also the lives of officials who are required to evacuate everyone. Until the people are evacuated, those rescuers will not be able to help fight the fire.

"We used every technique to tell people," Mike Fisher says. "[We told them to] forget the fire, get people out."

Most people think they will be able to keep from being

burned alive, but they may not think of other hazards in a massive forest fire. The official 2012 report on the Bastrop Complex Fire points out the hazards of staying in the fire zone. An average ground fire on the forest floor with flames three feet tall can be as hot as 1,472 degrees Fahrenheit. Under more extreme conditions—such as those present in Bastrop—temperatures can reach 2,192 degrees. Besides this obvious threat are more subtle dangers:

- Fire replaces oxygen, causing suffocation.
- Poisonous gases fill the air.
- Breathing in smoke can burn the insides of the lungs, harming gas exchange.
- Even if the flame does not reach a person, the *radiant heat* can cause serious burns from far away, overwhelming the body's cooling system.
- Fire attacks from all sides: falling embers, downed power lines, and deep burning holes.
- Propane is a hazard all its own. If propane is heated above 920 degrees Fahrenheit, it will ignite without a spark. The resulting fire will burn at over 3,000 degrees Fahrenheit, not an environment conducive to human survival, much less safety. Did propane tanks explode in the Bastrop Complex Fire? Many civilians believe they heard them exploding, but officials are not so sure.

It is possible for a propane tank to explode under tremendous amounts of sustained heat or pressure, which were definitely present in the Bastrop Complex Fire. However, propane tanks also have safety valves which will blow off under pressure, releasing the gas in a steady stream, normally emptying a propane tank before the proper temperature can be reached for an explosion.

At 4:30 in the afternoon, the motel where the firefighters parked was no longer safe, and they moved again. The central command post would now be in the city of Bastrop. Another fire had started north of the first fire. The wind was blowing this fire down to meet the first fire. When the two joined, the result would be even hotter and fiercer.

Mike Fisher was right. Not only did the people of Bastrop have enough common sense to save themselves, but many of them saved others as well. When he began to hear the evacuation stories, Mike realized that very few people were prepared to evacuate, but almost all were resourceful enough to do what they needed to do. Although many people didn't have time to grab a toothbrush, they knew where they were going and how to get out, and they drove through flames to do it.

Knowing he would be needed at the Emergency Operations Center (EOC), Mike headed back to Bastrop. He was glad to know that every method to warn people was in place. Dispatchers had activated reverse 9-1-1, and deputies were running from door to door on foot. All the workers were doing what they were trained to do. When he heard Josh's instruction for the firefighters to abandon their posts and escape for their lives, Mike declared the fire to be a disaster.

His advice to bring in an extra dispatcher was a good idea. The dispatchers in the windowless room had eight phone lines, and all eight were constantly full. Although they normally tracked all calls on the computer, the dispatchers finally gave up their keyboards and began to track the calls by hand, finding it faster than stopping to put their information into the computer. They also tried to keep up with what the firemen and police officers were doing, but they just couldn't do it all.

The dispatchers had no idea what the fire looked like, but from the radio traffic they could tell it was bad. Normally, the officers addressed each other in a professional manner, by their last names. When the dispatchers heard the officers calling each other by their first names over their radios, they knew the situation was serious.

Finally, after two hours of continuous calls, the dispatcher looked at her computer. There were four hundred abandoned calls. "I had a horrible sinking feeling," the dispatcher said. "It was just too much."

Then the dispatcher began receiving calls from friends and family. She told them to pick up their valuables and get out. Sadly, she realized there was no one at her house to do this for her.

A dreadful helplessness set in as the dispatcher realized that her house and all its contents might be gone. She stepped away from the ringing phones into the office kitchenette to be alone for a few seconds. After a moment of grieving, she went back to her job.

When Mike Fisher arrived back from Elgin on that Sunday afternoon, there were about twenty people gathered in the Bastrop County offices. Mike worked shoulder to shoulder with Judge McDonald, and they were joined by other city and county staff, making up the EOC. Their job consisted of making decisions, planning, and directing all aspects of the recovery effort. They arranged for supplies and resources, coordinated communication with the media, and made sure necessary messages were sent to everyone affected by the fire.

Gayle Wilhelm, the judge's secretary, was at a church function on Sunday when she began getting phone calls and hearing reports of a Bastrop fire. She wasn't especially alarmed because she had gotten many calls like this before. She expected the next call would be someone saying, "We're mopping up now."

Instead, Judge McDonald himself called her. "Come," he said. The abruptness of his message alarmed Gayle.

The judge himself had been planning to spend a relaxing day with the mayor when Mike Fisher called them and informed them of the state of affairs. The judge and the mayor looked at each other. "I don't think we're going anywhere today," they concluded. Soon they realized they wouldn't be relaxing for at least a whole week.

The traffic was chaotic as Gayle drove into town. She saw the swirling gray cloud of smoke over Bastrop.

In a few hours the number of people gathered with Mike Fisher and

Judge McDonald had swelled to eighty. News crews arrived, and the EOC allowed them to park in the large parking lot across the street between Coffee Dog and Super Donuts.

The EOC arranged for a helicopter to land in the parking lot outside Super Donuts. When it landed, Fire Chief Henry Perry climbed in. His job was to get a view of the fire and help with the organization of firefighting efforts. Rising above the Bastrop treetops, the chief saw a giant cloud where he would normally see the eastern sky. It was the cloud that Gayle saw as she drove to Bastrop. It was the cloud that Mike Fisher saw forming as he drove back from Elgin. It was the cloud that many of the residents of Bastrop could not see until they got out of the forest.

Beneath the nebulous gray mass on top were smaller, tighter spirals of white, shaped almost like tornadoes, but bending and swirling in the wind. The newest smoke was white, set against the gray haze of burning embers and soot-filled air. Below the clouds, the dark green of the loblolly pine forest stretched for miles, a bed of fuel. Each tree made its own little shape on the landscape, like a candle in the wind.

As the helicopter pilot circled the fire, Chief Perry saw orange appearing in and behind the smoke. Bursts of orange in black, like exploding bombs, rose high in the air, giving the whole sky an unearthly orange glow.

The second fire that had started north of the first fire had by now rushed south and caught up with the first fire. The two fires together were hotter and bigger than either had been by itself.

Had there been no wind, Chief Perry knew that the forest fire would have traveled slowly. It would have started as a surface fire and slowly spread through the woods. It would have burned the undergrowth before climbing the small trees. This heat on the forest floor would gradually have increased in temperature until the tall trees would finally have reached 140 degrees, when their rosin would turn into gas.

But there was strong wind. The fire from one torched tree spread to another tree close by, and that tree torched as well. Soon the combined heat was so great that no surface fire was needed to preheat the trees to 140 degrees. The fire was an independent crown fire. It would travel in the crowns of the trees until it ran out of fuel or the wind stopped.

The wind was traveling twenty-five miles per hour with gusts to forty miles per hour. By the time Chief Perry saw the fire from the sky, only hours after the first spark, the front of the fire had traveled like a thin snake all the way to the Colorado River ten miles away. It burned pathways through the Circle D subdivision, just missing the fire station. It burned down to Highway 21 and leaped across all four lanes. It burned into the state park, where the superintendent and his staff were frantically soaking the 75-year-old cabins and digging fire breaks. It seared a path to Highway 71 and jumped that four-lane highway also. Then it reached the Colorado River.

Perhaps the fire would not cross the river?

The wind wafted burning embers across the river. Some of them landed in people's yards far beyond the river. At the sale barn several miles away, where many evacuated animals were spending the night, chunks of bark fell from the sky. Sale barn employees, although accustomed to challenges such as heading off longhorns and wrestling with goats, worried about the enormous challenge of a possible evacuation of the sale barn.

Amazingly, the fire had not yet burned toward Tahitian Village, and it had spared many houses. It had not yet done much damage to the state park. It was still a relatively thin strip of fire, running fast and hot instead of widening. But it was not staying thin.

Although the wind pushed the fire south, the fire spread in all directions, creeping in the grass and leaping into shrubs and trees. Blowing embers out ahead of itself, it paved its own path of destruction.

Some of the burning embers fell into the whitecaps on Lake Bastrop and went out. Some of them dropped into the Colorado River and went out. Some also extinguished when they fell on highways or metal roofs.

But other embers dropped into eaves troughs full of pine needles and onto upholstered patio chairs. In the dryness and heat, these small flames curled up under the roofs and reached down to the decks, starting the houses on fire.

Looking down at the orange pillars of fire, Chief Perry knew that the dropping embers were not the only way to start houses on fire. In places where the heat was fiercest, the radiant heat would reach through the window glass. Even if the outside of the house were metal, the fire could start from the inside. Curtains, drapes, furniture, or artificial plants could catch fire.

Chief Perry looked down from the helicopter onto the wildland-urban interface with its thousands of trees and houses and people. The forest scar was beginning to widen with every mile into a giant teardrop shape. Those houses being surrounded by intense radiant heat . . . were people still in them?

The firefighters could not surround the fire. Even from the air, Chief Perry could not measure it. The fire had already forced his small band of well-trained volunteer firefighters to retreat. There was no stopping this monster. Although he could not see them, Chief Perry knew that his firefighters even now were running from door to door, knocking and yelling, making sure all the houses were empty. They were cutting fences and opening cages, allowing animals to run free.

It was easy to see why forest fires, which start in seconds, can burn for weeks. The chief knew that once help arrived from state and federal departments, they would be able to contain the fire somewhat. They would be able to map out the perimeter of the fire and begin building a fire line through the forest.

But putting out each flame would be impossible until the wind died, the humidity rose, and the temperature fell.

ANONYMOUS ESCAPE STORIES FROM THE BASTROP FIRE

An unknown motorist on Highway 21 picked up two ladies. One was an elderly lady with a walker. The other was her caretaker, who was using a cane since her recent knee surgery. The motorist found them at the side of Highway 21. Burning embers were falling around them in the smoke.

When they were safe in the vehicle, they told their story. Neither woman had heard about the fire. The caretaker decided to go outside to exercise her knee, but when she looked out the window, she saw ash falling. Smelling smoke, she opened the garage door to investigate and saw orange flame.

Quickly shutting the garage door, the caretaker concluded they would have to escape on foot through the backyard. She got the elderly lady up and outside, with her walker. She held onto her cane, and together they inched across the backyard, smoke swirling around them.

"You gotta go faster!" the caretaker said as they bumped over the rough terrain.

"I'm going as fast as I can," the elderly lady replied.

The caretaker heard an explosion. She realized that burning embers were falling from the sky. She looked at her clothes and saw a hole burned through the fabric.

"If you don't go faster, I'm going to throw you on my back," the caretaker threatened.

When they reached Highway 21 and caught a ride, the fire was right behind them.

A man alone in his house was aware of the fire, but he didn't think it was close to his house. He lay down for a nap. When he woke up, he saw an orange glow in all the windows and a wall of flame headed for his house. He grabbed his medicine, leaped into a vehicle, and drove out through flames. The *Bastrop Advertiser* reports that he did not know how he got out.

> One man had just bought a house in Bastrop. He was planning to sell his house just south of Bastrop to pay for the new one in Bastrop, after which he planned to move into the new house. When he heard that his Bastrop house was burning, he hurried up to investigate. He discovered it was a total loss and was greatly relieved that he had not moved his possessions up to the new house. While he was still in Bastrop, he got a call from his old neighborhood. His house south of Bastrop, which housed his possessions, was burning as well.

It got dark about 8:00. Against the dark skies, pine trees lit up like torches, and clouds of smoke glowed red. In the shadow of this column, thousands of feet high, smaller brush fires burned in every corner, lit by falling sparks. Explosions were heard as houses went up in smoke.

The cloud of smoke began to make its own weather. Small bursts of rain fell. New winds blew. Fire whirls, like glowing tornadoes, danced in the night sky.

Because the fire was more visible at night, it was easier to fight. The temperature cooled slightly. Still, the air remained hot and the wind continued to blow strong. The firefighters were exhausted. But they had the energy to fight on. They were fighting for their own houses and their own neighborhoods. When they got tired, all they needed to see was a burning pine cone dropping onto the roof of a friend's house, and their energy returned.

At midnight Josh Gill saw seven mutual aid fire trucks driving up the highway. Josh and his men were exhausted, soaked with sweat and plastered with soot. How exciting to see help arrive! Josh waved the crew in.

The drivers of the seven trucks sadly informed Josh that they were not allowed to stop. They were on duty for the next morning and were commanded to go sleep. The rigid rules of a massive firefighting effort were setting in, and for order to remain, the rules would have to be followed. Josh Gill and his firefighters would keep fighting through the night—alone.

Back in Bastrop, the brains organizing this massive effort were getting cramped. Mike and Judge McDonald quickly realized that their normal building was too small to be the headquarters for such an incident. Between 10:00 p.m. and midnight, they sealed a deal with the city to move the EOC to a 30,000-square-foot convention center. Besides being large enough to handle the EOC, it was slightly closer to the fire zone.

> ## WILDFIRE MECHANICS: TORCHING, CROWN FIRES, SPOTTING, AND CONVECTIVE COLUMNS
>
> *Torching* describes the astonishing process of the nearly instantaneous combustion of a tree, says William Cottrell, Jr. in *The Book of Fire*. If the torching involves a number of close trees, the fire can become a crown fire.
>
> Torching is the second phase of the fire process, called the ignition phase. A tree will not just spontaneously combust without some pre-ignition phase, some warming from above or below. Usually in a forest fire, the fire creeps up through ground fuels, driven by the wind. The more plentiful the surface fuels, the more chance they will cause the whole tree to ignite. This is where the term *ladder fuel* is used. Ladder fuels enable a ground fire to climb into the treetops. Perhaps a dead tree has fallen and is leaning on several live trees. The fire climbs up the dead tree like a ladder before exploding into the treetops. The ladder fuel could be smaller trees or shrubs, such as bushes covered with old pine needles.
>
> Since there is usually a wind in these cases, an interesting

thing happens to the trunks of the trees. The invisible cloud of gas (vaporized rosin) that seeps out of a pine tree is pushed by the wind to the side of the trunk *away from* the wind. This concentrated pipeline of gas on the downwind side of the tree can also become a ladder for the fire. The fire climbs up the downwind side of the tree and rushes into the cloud of gas in the tree tops. It is possible, following a forest fire, to tell which way the wind was blowing just by observing the trunks of the trees.

If there is not a lot of wind, the surface fire will continue to creep through the ground fuel, warming the forest floor before climbing into the treetops and creating crown fires. If there *is* a strong wind, such as in Bastrop on Labor Day weekend, the crown fire can continue to travel through the tops of the trees on its own, without the preheating from the surface fire. This is called an *independent crown fire.*

A forest fire can spread in other ways besides the impressive crown fire. As long as the surface fire has fuel, it will continue to spread. A *heading fire* moves with the wind and therefore moves most quickly. However, the fire can also move backwards, into the wind, as long as there is fuel available to back into. This is called a *backing fire.* In addition, the fire will move off to the sides at a medium speed. This is called a *flanking fire.*

A more unpredictable way a forest fire spreads is through spotting. This occurs when the wind lofts burning fuels out ahead of the fire. Depending on where they land, they will either be extinguished or start a new fire. The stronger the wind, the farther the firebrands will travel and the greater the endangered area will be.

Not only does the fire spread in all directions on the ground, its effects also spread upward. Because heat rises, the hot air from the fire creates a column that rushes up into the sky past the cooler air around it. The column of hot air, called a convective column, is full of smoke, water vapor from the burning fuels, and fiery brands. The hot air will not stop rising until it cools to the temperature of the air around it, and this may be 40,000 feet high.[2] There, the water vapor condenses and forms a fluffy white cloud which may produce its own rain. Regional weather can be affected by a large forest fire.

With all the hot air swirling up, the cloud may produce other weather: hurricane-like winds and fire whirls similar to tornadoes.[a] Trees may be ripped out by the roots, and branches and burning bark might soar high into the sky. At its most powerful point, a forest fire can produce as much energy as an atomic bomb every five to fifteen minutes.[3]

The strong wind that often fans a forest fire continues to pressure the column of hot air. Normally, the convective column will be strong enough that the wind will just pass around it on either side. If the wind is strong enough to actually break open the column of hot air, extreme destruction occurs. All of the burning brands that would have otherwise burned out high in the air are instead propelled forward, dropping up to a mile ahead of the fire at a rate of thousands per acre.[4]

---

[a] See third photo in photo section.

10

THE NIGHT NO ONE SLEPT

It was a holiday weekend—normally a time to sleep in and have cookouts, a time for afternoon naps and reading the newspaper. Instead, Bastrop's Labor Day of 2011 would be a day of physical, mental, and emotional labor.

For the firefighters, it was physical labor all night long without sleep. As Josh Gill realized when the fire first started, fighting each flame was completely impossible. They had to evacuate people, minimize destruction, and think of their own safety.

To stay safe, they had to know how to communicate clearly with each other. They could not casually rush into a fire zone because the fire could jump over them and trap them suddenly. Smoke could settle in and blind them, as it did when they first tried to evacuate from the Circle D area.

Later in the evening it happened again. A brush truck drove from Cardinal Lane onto a back road because there had been rumors that someone was still in a house there. Then the smoke settled in and they could see nothing. They had no idea how to get back out to Cardinal Lane.

They radioed to the engine that had been closest to them. The engine drivers took the address of the brush truck and drove down the back road to try to find it. Using the radio, the two trucks agreed to blast their air horns to communicate. The engine drivers finally heard the air horn of the brush truck, even though they still could not see it. They parked the engine in the middle of the road and ran on foot into the lane toward the sound of the air horn. With their help, the brush truck was finally able to find its way out.[1]

As neighborhoods cleared out, firefighters switched from evacuating people to fighting the fire. Josh Gill, Alan Donaldson, George Martinez, and the rest of the firefighters began the hard work of fighting the wildfire by hand. Because the people were safe, they focused on saving the houses and animals.

They worked to save the houses by taking fuel away from them. They divided into small groups and spread throughout the burning area. They swept pine needles off roofs with brooms. They used shovels and axes to chop away undergrowth that might lead the fire to a building. They hurled lawn chairs out of backyards and threw patio umbrellas off decks.

The firefighters rescued many animals. They broke windows and pulled pets out, tagging the animals with a piece of tape with their address. The men chopped down fences, letting horses, cattle, and emus run free. They lifted the lids off parrot cages so the birds were free to escape.

For Mike Fisher, Judge McDonald, and their staff, Labor Day weekend was full of mental labor. They moved all their supplies, maps, and computers out of their offices and hauled them under the gray stucco archways and orange brick of the convention center. They arranged laptops and plastic file boxes on round tables. They separated the convention center into orderly areas so each department and committee could have its own space. They planned for the many other people who would arrive in the next few days as word of the disaster spread and assistance arrived.

Throughout the night of September 4, they kept track of what was happening in the fire zone. Following protocol, they also needed to plan out the next day before that day even arrived. They had to be sure there were firefighters ready to replace the exhausted locals. They had to make sure there would be staff around the clock for the next week to answer the civilians' questions.

Judge McDonald and Mike Fisher hoped the death toll from the fire would not be high, but they could not imagine anything else. They arranged for refrigerated trucks and body bags. As much as they dreaded the thought, with a fire of such force, they were sure they would need these supplies. They ordered cadaver dogs to scout through the burn area and asked for a portable mortuary.

As Judge McDonald's secretary, Gayle Wilhelm was responsible for dealing with the media on a day-to-day basis. Usually the job of public information officer was only a side responsibility for her. Safe behind her desk outside the judge's chambers, surrounded by white walls, gray carpet, and plants with trailing vines, she could satisfy the media with an email or phone call.

Now she was dealing with news stations calling and wondering where they could park their trucks. Sometimes the news vehicles just showed up and demanded attention. On the afternoon of the fourth, she had finally sent them across the street to the parking lot in front of Super Donuts, empty for the holiday. Through the night of September 4, she debated how to handle their demands for information.

The media announcements could be useful. She knew all the displaced citizens of Bastrop would hang onto every word about the disaster. Should she just pass on every bit of information she heard? Or should she wait, while people were becoming impatient, and double-check the information to make sure it was totally accurate? It was like walking on a reporter's fence with speed on one side and accuracy on the other. She had to stay in the middle.

For the citizens evacuated to the shelters or to the over-filled homes of relatives, it was a day of emotional labor. They wondered if their homes were burning. They wondered if friends and family were safe. Although many of the citizens were able to find beds, few slept well that night. At the shelters, children were sleeping on makeshift pallets. Sleeping bags were strewn everywhere. A trip to the toilet carried the risk of stepping on someone. Most of the adults were awake, thinking, their eyes boring holes in the darkness.

With the smell of smoke still embedded in their senses, the people dreamt restlessly, picturing their favorite clothes, computers and printers, collectibles, antiques, photo albums, and projects burning. They wondered about the vehicles they had left behind, as well as their pets. They imagined smoke creeping over their property, growing thicker, and suddenly bursting into orange flame. They wondered if their propane tanks were exploding, their tools and farm equipment melting into pools of glossy metal or burning into rusty skeletons. They wondered if the rumors were true—had Terry's Corner, the gas station acting as a meeting place for evacuees, really gone up in flames?

Debra lay awake at a friend's house, thinking of the house that God built. Was it still standing under the pines? What about the trampoline where she would grow dizzy looking at the tops of the pines against the stars? What about the one lone oak tree and the family pickle swing dangling from it? At their departure, the trees had been bending ominously, the pickle swing whipping wildly in the wind.

Debra remembered how the house had come into their lives right after she and her husband had become Christians. Their house had been like a classroom, teaching them how to trust God.

She had learned the art of hospitality in that house. Debra had grown up in New England where company was not invited unless the house was perfectly dusted and vacuumed and at least a day's notice was given. In her growing up years, a knock on the door caused everyone in the house to freeze and ask each other, "Did someone call and say they were coming over?" Upon acquisition of their ragged trailer, Debra had definitely not considered herself to be a good candidate for a hostess.

After she became a Christian, Debra started attending a women's Bible study hosted by her pastor's wife. They were discussing spiritual gifts when they came to "hospitality."

"I don't have that one," Debra said with relief. She was glad that she didn't have to practice hospitality.

The pastor's wife encouraged her that the intention of the Bible was that, even if she didn't have a certain gift, she was still called to do the best she could in that area. She explained it might just be more difficult for the person who doesn't have that spiritual gift.

"Do you think the Lord expects me to open my house in the broken-down condition it's in?" Debra wondered, shocked. She felt so embarrassed about her house. It was small, old, and easily cluttered.

With time, Debra did learn the skill of hospitality. Her best friend Holly showed her how. Holly's house could be a total wreck, but she would still welcome people in. The party was always at Holly's.

Waving her New England alarm into the background, Debra was finally able to say, "Move the laundry and have a seat. I'll get you a glass of tea."

As Debra had grown comfortable with hospitality, she had begun to long for space to have more company. She and Dean had wished they could host Bible studies. Their pastor's wife, bound to a scooter or walker, could visit the Pahlow home only with great difficulty. With steep stairs and skinny doors, their home wasn't readily accessible.

But now, as Debra lay awake the night of September 4, she realized that she might not have a house at all.

Mike Gibbons took his mother to a community shelter. For a while, the shelters were mass confusion. There was no food or water. Children were separated from their parents. Some of the children, not understanding what was going on, were excited and almost giddy with the sudden activity. Some people were hysterical.

Mike Gibbons was glad he had brought his mother out to safety, but he was beginning to regret having evacuated himself. He knew the Bastrop Fire Department would be stretched thin and definitely could not defend property. Mike thought of Itsatown and the years of family labor it represented. He determined to go back into the fire zone and defend it himself.

Meanwhile, Mike's wife Shirley paced the Albuquerque airport, waiting for a flight back to Bastrop. It took her eight hours to find one. Those were the longest airport hours she would ever spend. She could not get in contact with Mike, who must have forgotten either his cell phone or his charger.

Finally she got on a flight to Austin. When they approached to land, she looked out the window in the direction of Bastrop. It was Monday morning already, and sunlight was falling over the Texan countryside.

Normally when she looked out, all she could see was a massive patch of pine green, which she knew was the forest of the Lost Pines. Somewhere in that forest, she knew her house was tucked under the trees, under the windmill, beside Itsatown and all their family treasures.

Now she saw a cloud of dirty brown smoke as high as the airplane. Beneath it, etched in the green, was a massive black scar.

Wesley and Margaret ate supper at their church with other church members. Then they spent the night at Jerry's house, one of their twins. Margaret had no idea if their house was burning. From Jerry's house, she looked toward the forest. She could not see flames, but she saw a tremendous cloud of smoke. Under the cloud, the sky was red.

Wesley and Margaret also had trouble sleeping that night. The things in their house were just things, they knew. The house itself was just a thing. The cake topper from their wedding, the souvenirs from Central America, and Margaret's favorite oak tree were just things.

But all the things were attached to memories. All the things were symbolic of different parts of their lives. As Margaret looked back over the decades, she realized that their most valuable things were the ones that had taught them about God.

The oak tree had always reminded her that God was good. The cedar chest from their dating years and their fiftieth anniversary picture reminded her that God was faithful. He had been with them all those decades.

The stools from Southwestern Bell Telephone Company and the rice china from Panama were symbolic of a rougher time in life. Margaret had resented Wesley's trips to construct houses for the poor in Central America. The twins were sixteen, and because Wesley used all his vacation time for missions, none was left for quality family time. His trips had cost a lot too.

Wesley always returned with souvenirs and stories. He told of islands off the Bahamas that had no fresh water. He told of the islanders' unique cultural practices, such as their monetary system based on coconuts. He told of how, after finishing a chicken meal, he would set the bones down only to have long brown arms reach over, grab the drumsticks, and pick them over some more.

Even though Margaret was glad he was helping people, the expense of the trips annoyed her. Then she noticed an interesting pattern. Whenever Wesley returned from a mission trip, he would get lots of overtime hours at work. It was so consistent that Margaret could do nothing but praise God as the big paychecks arrived. She realized that even though Wesley had given up his vacation to serve God, he couldn't out-give God. God always blessed him back.

In time, Margaret warmed to the idea. She began to go with her husband on his trips. Several times Margaret and Wesley flew to Managua, the capital of Nicaragua, during times of war and communist control.

Only later did Margaret realize how dangerous their trips were. The Sandinistas and Contras were fighting at the time, and nothing could be purchased in the upper-class Managuan stores if you were not a card-carrying Communist.

However, God out-gave them again. There was no denying the unexplainable miracles that surrounded these trips. There was no way to forget them either.

Lying awake at night, Margaret remembered the time the water and electricity had been shut off. A small Nicaraguan boy said, "I know where there's water." He showed them a faucet in a field. They filled containers with the water from the faucet. When they returned a few days later, no faucet could be found there.

Margaret remembered another time when she had met a stranger in the Managua airport. Because of the war, the airport was cloaked with black curtains. "God, please don't let them open our luggage," Margaret prayed. It was against the law to bring in food, and Margaret knew the airport officials might be only too happy to destroy their things.

Suddenly a man walked over to her. "Are you Margaret?" he had asked, indicating that he was to assist her. She gratefully accepted his help, assuming the mission had sent him. He asked where her husband was, and she explained that he was waiting on his construction level in the baggage claim area.

The stranger spoke to the customs man in Spanish, and the customs man allowed Margaret through without question. When she turned around to thank the stranger, he was gone.

The miracles had not only happened once. Whenever Wesley and Margaret gave their time to God, God out-gave them.

Their house in the Lost Pines was full of memorials to those times.

Patty Timmons and her husband, with their dog Shadow, retreated to a La Quinta hotel on the way to Austin. The hotel was graciously allowing the evacuees to bring their animals also. As they settled in, Patty watched the eastern sky. The cloud of smoke was monstrous.

Patty thought of her cats at home. She thought of the scrapbook of her father's photos. Was the house filling with smoke? Even at the hotel, smoke hung in the air outside.

La Quinta was filled with other Bastrop residents and their pets, and Patty was able to hear stories of the fire from other perspectives. She felt much better knowing they were not the only ones.

After escaping from the fire zone and treating their grandchildren to pizza, Adam and Cindy also drove toward Austin to find a motel. After checking in, Cindy went to the ice machine. There she met several other Bastrop evacuees.

Though Cindy didn't expect to sleep a wink that night, it was good to know they were among friends.

After the failed attempt to sneak back to their house, Nicholas and his wife retreated to her family.

Lying awake that night, Nicholas thought about his dog, Ranger, alone in his small log cabin. He thought about their house, loaded with valuable educational artifacts.

Nicholas also remembered their recent study of the book of Job. The first chapter explained how Job, a wealthy man, had lost all his possessions on one day. Bandits had killed his oxen and camels. Fire had destroyed his sheep and their shepherds. A tornado had killed his children as they feasted at their oldest brother's house. Through it all, Job had refused to give up his trust in God.

Nicholas and his wife wondered . . . would their own faith in God be that strong if they lost everything? They had their minivan and the clothes on their backs—that was all.

After making sure that their son and his cousin were safely out of the fire zone, Efrain and Debi retreated to Debi's sister's house. By the end of the night, there were twenty-two refugees at her house. Even Efrain and Debi's elderly neighbor, whom their son had pulled from his house in a daze, ended up there. Since the people far outnumbered the beds, they all tried to make themselves as comfortable as possible on couches and sleeping bags.

Efrain made a trip to Walmart. He couldn't believe what they had forgotten to grab. He had no toothbrush. They had their cat but no cat food. As he made out a list, other people added requests onto it.

They tried to sleep that night, but helicopters pounded overhead. At least they felt safely out of the fire zone. They were on the other side of Bastrop, away from the fire.

Alan Donaldson did not evacuate the fire zone—he fought it with the other Bastrop firefighters. Despite the monstrosity of the fire, he found himself amazed at its beauty. Everything glowed. There were millions of points of light, small fires sprouting everywhere. As he had done before, he looked up for the matching points of light, the expanse of reflecting stars. But this time, there were no stars, only a rolling smoke cap with glowing patches of orange, always changing, rising, and swirling in the wind.

Well, there goes my house, he thought.

As the firefighting took him close to his own house, he looked toward it through the inferno. He wasn't sure exactly where it was. He had lived there for seventeen years, but now he couldn't recognize anything. Finally he was fairly certain he was close to his house. He knew where it should be; and he knew that if it was still there, it would be a black shape in the darkness, blocking his view. Instead, Alan could see dancing fires far beyond the house site.

It was gone, along with his rooms of books, the Egyptian scarab beetle, and his Asian souvenirs. But he didn't have time to mourn; there was too much to do.

> ## HOW TO LEAVE THE HOUSE WHEN EVACUATING
> Wildfire plans instruct civilians to take down lightweight curtains, move furniture to the center of the room, and close metal shutters before leaving if they are not in imminent danger.
>
> The same plans ask residents to turn off all air conditioning, gas valves, and pilot lights, but to leave their lights on and their doors unlocked. If darkness falls, a lighted house will be easily seen by firefighters and therefore more readily protected. Unlocked doors allow firefighters to make sure no one is at home without breaking the door.

René Rizk and his wife and son spent the night at the home of their married son. Even though it was good to spend time with their son, daughter-in-law, and granddaughter, it was hard not to think about fearful things.

As the night stretched long, the only news they heard of the fire was that it was getting worse and spreading. It was hard to believe that only twelve hours before, the world had been a stable, familiar place.

After watching the fire for several hours from the hill close to Home Depot, Bill and Patsy realized they would not be going home for the night. They headed in the direction of Austin for a motel.

There, Patsy wanted to try to get some sleep. Bill, however, could not be caged in a motel room when fire was raging around his property. After lying awake for a few hours, he finally got up and told Patsy he was heading back. He sneaked back through the darkness toward their house. Before he was stopped by officials, he was stopped by the heavy smoke. He could not even drive up the street toward their house. He backed off to Highway 21 and sat there, determined to wait it out. However, he was finally discovered by emergency personnel, who told him to leave.

He left, but he was determined to go back later. Although she couldn't stop wondering what was happening, Patsy was content to be at a distance.

Jimmy Mack and his wife did not sleep much that night. They were glad they had their cat, but they had almost nothing else. As Jimmy lay awake, he made plans to go to Maxine's in the morning. Surely the restaurant would open. It would be a great place to meet his coffee buddies and share stories. A couple of twelve-inch griddle cakes might make things better too.

George Martinez's wife and two sons had evacuated the back way as they had practiced, avoiding the hour-long traffic jam of people trying to get out on Tahitian Drive. George himself returned to Tahitian Village with a band of firefighters. Although the fire had not directly hit Tahitian Village, the air was filled with burning embers, which were starting fires everywhere.

With eight fire trucks, they fought the spot fires in the subdivision. The terrain in Tahitian Village made firefighting extremely difficult.

Steep hills and deep gullies trapped and fed the fires while keeping them out of the reach of the fire trucks.

Fire climbs hills much more quickly than it can travel across flat land, because the fuel is easier to reach. The large flame literally leans up against more fuel. In contrast, fire has a much harder time traveling downhill. Forest fires often taper down or die out at the top of a mountain because they have difficulty traveling down the other side.

By midnight, the fires had still not crossed Tahitian Drive. The eighteen firefighters in the eight trucks fought on. None of the twelve hundred houses had been lost, and that was the important thing. There were burning embers flying through the air, but the houses were still standing. "Everything was glowing," George remembers. "The wind was blowing through things. It would just glow."

After everyone evacuated from Tahitian Village, the area became quiet except for the emergency workers. The firefighters gave Tahitian Village Market permission to stay open as long as it was safe.

Tahitian Village Market was a strategic asset to the firefighters in their battle. It became an oasis. Ryan Terranova and his mother filled coolers with ice and drinks. They pumped gallons of gas for the fire trucks all through the evening and into the night. While the firefighters filled their tanks, they would ask for Gatorade, snacks, or ice. Ryan ran into the store to get the things they ordered so they would not have to waste the time and energy.

After nearly everyone had evacuated, a civilian arrived at the station with a five-gallon gas can. He said his wife was still back in Tahitian Village, confined to a wheelchair. They had a handicap accessible van, but it was out of gas. The man had forgotten his money, but Ryan pumped the five gallons for him anyway.

Besides supplying food, water, gas, and ice to the emergency personnel, Ryan became the "operator" for all his friends who lived in or near Tahitian Village. They knew that he was still inside the fire zone, and they called him all through the night to see what was happening. Ryan took care of the store while his mother went to take a nap.

At 4:00 a.m., Ryan's mother returned from her nap, and Ryan went to try to get some sleep. But, like everyone else in Bastrop that night, he had trouble sleeping.

PHOTO SECTION

PHOTO SECTION

PHOTO SECTION

PHOTO SECTION

PHOTO SECTION

PHOTO SECTION

© Henry Perry

PHOTO SECTION

The wall of smoke as seen by Chief Perry and others in the helicopter.

PHOTO SECTION

Damaged but recognizable, "The Eye of the Storm" metal cross stands prominently in a burned-out stump in the Pahlows' front yard.

With the help of water from a 20,000-gallon tank, the Gibbons' family museum, Itsatown, and its contents were spared.

PHOTO SECTION

Work on Wesley and Margaret Peschke's new house begins against the background of a blackened forest.

A few of Patty Timmons' sun catchers—green and blue gemstones skillfully enclosed in artistic frameworks of rusted wire found in the fire debris.

Alan Donaldson loved to read, but not when there was a fire to fight!

PHOTO SECTION

Adam and Cindy Cruz lost their house but not their faith.

A burnt page from Nicholas Cowey's hymnal collection.

PHOTO SECTION

Bill and Patsy Ludwig's cedar bench, handcrafted from a large tree destroyed in the fire.

Larry Miller lost many of his specialty goats in the fire, but enough survived to rebuild his herd.

PHOTO SECTION

George Martinez, volunteer Bastrop firefighter in Tahitian Village.

Chief Henry Perry, Bastrop's head fire chief, viewed the fire from the air and helped organize firefighting efforts.

District Chief Josh Gill was the first firefighter to arrive on the scene.

PHOTO SECTION

Mike Fisher, Bastrop County's emergency management coordinator, worked tirelessly to keep people informed and educated.

The cast iron firefighter outside Fire Station #1 in downtown Bastrop.

PHOTO SECTION

District Chief William Laird, who kindly supplied striking fire photos for this book in addition to fighting the fire for the first 22 hours.

The intense heat melted street lights.

A house completely destroyed— as if a bomb had exploded.

PHOTO SECTION

Remains of a house and several vehicles in a blackened forest—proof of what had been a populated forest community.

People look at the list of destroyed homes,
hoping they will not see their own.

PHOTO SECTION

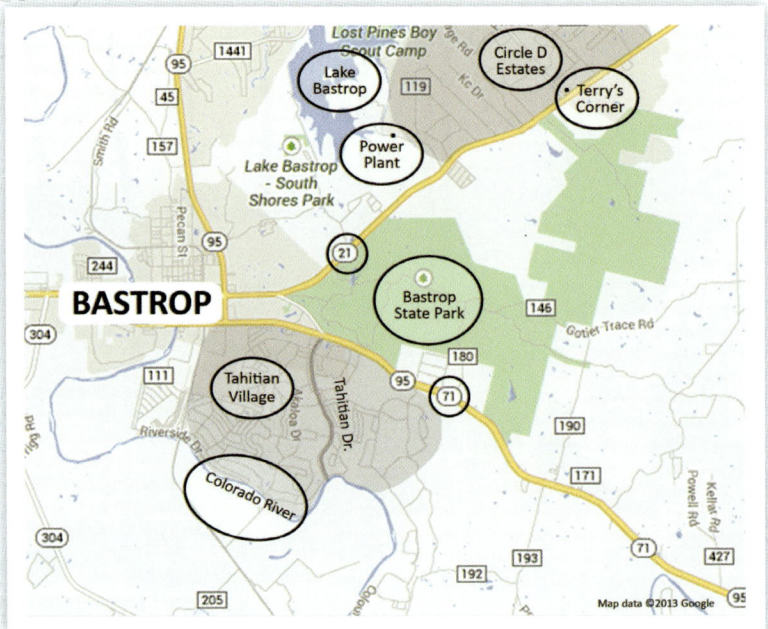

The Bastrop Complex Fire began in the Circle D Estates and blazed south across two main highways to the Colorado River, destroying many homes and loblolly pines in the beautiful wildland-urban interface.

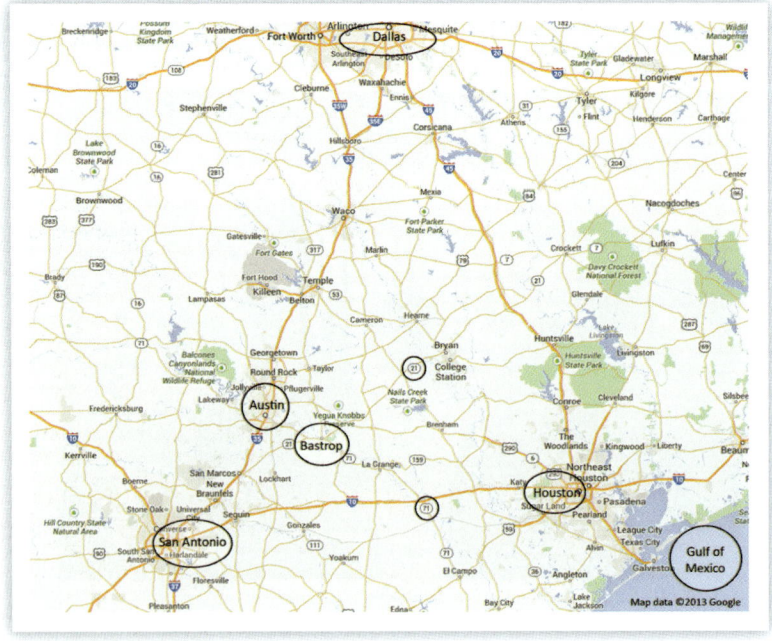

Bastrop lies within the triangle formed by Texas' three largest cities—Houston, San Antonio, and Dallas.

11

DAY OF LABOR

Finally the word got out. Everyone knew about a really big fire in Bastrop. Because of the mixed stories about the fire, no one knew exactly how bad it was or how many houses had burned. But everyone for miles around could see the cloud.

Instead of stopping overnight, the fire had barely slowed. By Monday morning, the sun rose again, as hot and bright as ever. The people in Bastrop could see its light, but they could not see the sun. All they could see was a glow behind the massive gray cloud.

Finally, help began to arrive. Chief Perry knew that his firefighters had been fighting all night without sleep. Now that there was backup, the chief called his men back to Station #1 about 10:00 a.m.

As he waited for them to arrive, the chief looked at the wall that had become the guestbook for the Bastrop Fire Department. At the top of the wall, sketched with a black marker, were mountain peaks with a river descending from them. At the end of the river was a symbol of the state of Texas. Under the stick figure Rockies were words that read, "Northern Colorado Engine Strike Team, 1998." Lined up on either side of the river were hand-sketched seals of the various fire departments represented from Boulder, Colorado. Names of personnel were listed beneath each seal. In a different hand, a single name was scrawled nearby: "Justin Donbronski, 1999, Back Again!" Nearby, another guestbook entry said, "Tropical Storm Charlie, 8-22-98."

Some of the guestbook entries on the wall were done with colored markers. Others were black and white. Some were done with perfect symmetry, and others were distinctly free-hand. The wall was like a game of I-Spy. Upon close inspection, Chief Perry could find local names: Mike Fisher and Josh Gill. There was a sketch of an alligator complete with scales, a shaded underbelly, and teeth, labeled "Florida Wildland Firefighters." There was a helicopter shaped like an armadillo. Under the armadillo were the words, "If it's a dry heat, why am I sweating?"

Chief Perry shook his head. He knew the guestbook would have many new entries in the next days. He walked to his office with its walls of plaques and awards, its fire hats, mugs, and fat binders. There he would wait for his firefighters.

They began to arrive at the brick station on Chestnut Street, grim-faced and dirty. Beside them, the metal firefighter statue stood on his brick pedestal, holding the child he had rescued. Behind the statue was the massive gray cloud.

The local firefighters had been fighting for about twenty hours. Despite their minor injuries, coating of soot, and extreme exhaustion, many of the firefighters were upset about being asked to leave the fire lines. They had formed the lines and tirelessly defended them all night, beating back the fire from their own houses or the houses of neighbors and friends. They did not want to give their job to men from California or Alaska.

Some, like Alan, knew that their houses were lost. Others, like Josh Gill, had fought the fire on his own street. When he left Monday morning, seven of the thirty homes on his street had burned. His was still standing.

All of them had personal interest in the fire, much more than the people arriving from around the nation. Some even cursed Chief Perry for calling them back. However, the next day, after some sleep, most of them apologized.

The Bastrop firefighters were asked to be on call for normal house fires or emergencies that might arise in town. Still, as the days went on, it was hard to watch out-of-state people fight the Bastrop Fire.

"This is our fire!" the men said. The younger firefighters were especially frustrated, but they did as they were told and stayed to answer the local calls. Grateful residents made sure the firefighters had food to eat every day.

> ### STATE AND FEDERAL TEAMS
> Texas Forest Service gained recognition in 2003 after the crash of the *Columbia* space ship because their method of handling disasters was so efficient. Because they are skilled at dealing with emergencies, the forest service gets called upon to direct disasters unrelated to the forest. Because the Bastrop fire was so severe, a national team named the Southern Area Red Team was called in. This federal team is a Type 1 team, the highest-caliber team available.
>
> The nation's wildland firefighting system is the best in the world. The United States has a massive database listing all the wildland firefighters in the country with their qualifications. When a state or region gets stressed beyond its own resources, they call to the closest Geographical Area Coordination (GAC) office. The GAC office notifies the closest region in the database, letting the firefighters know what roles are needed. As the needs are filled, the database registers it.
>
> If the closest region doesn't supply enough help, the GAC office reaches farther, in ever-widening circles to more and more of the nation, asking for more help.

Paul Pellegrini, a firefighting crew leader from Alaska, had been in central Texas for several weeks already. The people on his crew were from all over the nation. Their equipment included bulldozers from Michigan and California as well as fire engines from Arizona and from South Dakota. There was one Texas Forest Service engine in the crew, but it was being manned by firefighters from the east coast.

On Sunday, September 4, Paul and his crew were fighting another bad fire in central Texas. The fire was threatening a few houses and attacking a historic train trestle. After fighting the fire all day, they went to sleep for the required eight hours. The professional fire crews guided their working hours by a 2 to 1 ratio. They fought the fire for sixteen hours and slept eight hours.

On Monday morning Paul and his crew woke up to the news that they were not supposed to go back to protect the train trestle. Instead, they were to report to "this place called Bastrop."

In Bastrop, Paul found a huge fire with not enough people to fight it. There they would have no 2 to 1 ratio, at least not right away. For the first several days in Bastrop, eight hours of sleep would seem like a distant memory.

Near Fire Station #1, the leaders of the EOC drew up huge paper maps of the Bastrop Complex Fire. Even though they still didn't know its exact boundaries, they knew that defining the location of the wildfire was the first step in dealing with it. They knew they could not stop the fire until they had a boundary line to defend.

The Bastrop Complex Fire was spreading over thirty thousand acres. Measuring around the edge of the fire, the commanders found that the fire line they needed to defend was fifty-four miles long. They would have to divide those fifty-four miles into small sections that groups of firefighters could watch and manage.

First, the fifty-four-mile perimeter was divided into two branches. Branch I was the northern part of the fire and Branch II was the southern part. Then the branches were divided into divisions, labeled with letters of the alphabet. On the western side of the fire, the side toward Bastrop, there was Division A, Division D, Division G, Division I, and on around the bottom of the fire counterclockwise back to Division Z at the top. The planners deliberately skipped letters. That way, for example, if the fire between A and D suddenly became much worse and needed to be divided into more sections, there were still letters left to use.

With the large fire line now broken into eleven divisions, things were already easier to manage. Now, instead of directing crews to go "fight the fire," they could be directed to focus their skills on a small portion of the boundary line. However, each division was still an average of five miles long.

If natural boundaries like roads and rivers could be used, the firefighters would have less work. In Bastrop, there were two four-lane highways cutting through the forest, but the fire had already crossed them. At the bottom of the forest the Colorado River made an excellent boundary line. The fire had already crossed it in some places, but the river would keep ground fires from spreading. And, the land across the river was grassland. It burned, but it was much easier to stop.

Where no natural or manmade boundary was available, the firefighters needed to make fire lines. Even civilians helped. In the grasslands across the Colorado River, farmers helped by plowing strips in the wide brown fields. When the fire burned up to the freshly turned soil, it extinguished.

Bulldozers created part of the boundary line, hauling away large bites of brush. In the places where bulldozers could not get through, the firefighters dug the boundary lines by hand. Sometimes they dug and chopped away brush. Sometimes they carefully burned the fuel away.

"Even today, with all the amazing advancements in machinery and technology, most of firefighting is still tough, dirty manual labor," says Taylor Morrison in his book *Wildfire*.[1]

When the firefighters built a fire line by hand, they split into groups. The first people in the crew carried chain saws to cut away small trees or wood. The next wave of people hurled the debris out of the way. Another wave followed, digging and scraping all the way down to the mineral soil on the forest floor, which would not burn. These ground crews were affectionately known as "ground pounders." Before the end of the Bastrop Complex Fire, there would be four hundred crew members ground pounding at once.

When the fire boundary line had been created by removing all the fuel, the firefighters widened the line by burning the fuel leading up to it.

Paul Pellegrini and his fellow firefighters, wearing yellow safety hats and heavy coats, used drip torches to start the controlled burns. The drip torches had special loops to keep the flame from backing up into the torch. The fuel, four parts diesel and one part gasoline, dripped out of the torch onto a lighted wick. Flaming globs of fire dropped to the forest floor, lighting the ground fuel that they wanted to burn away.

Paul was experienced. Because he was a crew leader, multi-tasking was necessary for productivity and communication. He held his torch in one hand and a communication radio in the other, smoke from the controlled burn wafting around him. The smoke and heat from the "real" fire was never far away.

Firefighters also started controlled burns on a small scale around homes to burn up any fuel that might provide a bridge from the burning forest to the structure. They soaked lawns with hoses to create a wet line, which would also stop the ground fire.

The huge power plant next to Lake Bastrop got special attention. Firefighters soaked the grass around it with water. Even though it was just a little to the west of the main fire, the spot fires and ground fires were burning every direction. The firefighters did not want to leave even the slightest chance for a spark to ignite the power plant, full of chemicals.

FIGHTING FIRE WITH FIRE

Firefighters are careful when they start a controlled fire. They wait until the wind is blowing *toward* the main fire. Then they walk together in a row, lighting parallel lines of

> fire with their torches. The firefighter farthest downwind walks ahead of the person beside him, so there will be no chance that his comrade's fire will put him in danger.[2]

Across Texas and the rest of the United States, volunteers heard about the fire. Stan Miller, part of Christian Aid Ministries' disaster response team, received a text at 7:29 a.m., Monday, September 5, from another team member who lived close to Bastrop.

"There is a major fire going east of Bastrop . . . should we be looking into this to see if we can be of any help in cleanup?"

Stan replied, "I think that would be something we should check into. Are you all okay? I heard it was close to you."

For Stan, the text would be the beginning of a long ministry to the people of Bastrop.

Downtown, Maxine's opened Monday morning, Labor Day. People choked the restaurant. It became the meeting place, the place to hear and tell fire stories. The dining area became packed with people, and the employees were in a hectic state. The fire had greatly affected Maxine's staff: fourteen employees, including the manager, had lost their homes.

The regulars were all there, sitting around the table in their campfire-side fashion. But this week they did some things out of the ordinary. With a burst of inspiration, several of the old-timers leaped up and began to help pour coffee and pass out menus. They even took drink orders, easing the stress on the employees for a few minutes.

All the while, as people packed Maxine's tables and crowded the EOC and drove in from out of state, the sun beat down, the wind blew, and the fire burned. As people camped out at shelters and the homes of relatives and friends, no end to the ravenous fire was in sight. Instead, the fire beneath the stunning cloud in the sky continued to expand.

Debra and her family had left their neighborhood, but one neighbor had sneaked back to the area. He was talking on the phone with Debra on Monday.

"I can see your house. Everything's good. The fire seems to be pretty far away," he assured her.

He was wrong. The fire was burning through the back woods toward Debra's house, leaping from tree to tree.

Ten minutes later he called back. "I see the smoke. It's in your backyard."

Ten minutes later he called again. "I can't see your house anymore. I have to go."

Debra could only imagine what she could not see. The fire crawled up the back lawn. It leaped into the tall pine trees and lit them like a dozen torches. The fire traveled toward the lone oak tree and the pickle swing swaying in the wind and heat. It dropped burning pine cones through the smoke onto the trampoline, where they melted holes in the black canvas.

The fire leaped onto the mobile home. It melted plastic like candle wax. It exhaled stinking black smoke as it roasted wood, vinyl, and steel together. Inside, it flamed high in the furniture and carpet. Debra's metal-work cross with the hurricane background, the gift from her student, was now truly in the "Eye of the Storm."

Back at her friend's house, Debra felt quite certain that her house was gone. She went out by herself for a walk down by the pond and spent a moment of anguish before the Lord. Then she composed herself and went to do the next thing.

The fire continued down Alum Creek Drive, destroying almost every home. Only one neighboring mobile home did not burn. The vinyl siding melted and ran down the side of the home, hanging together like spaghetti, but the building never ignited.

Crossing Highway 21, the fire beat a path toward the little white church and the sign with its encouraging words. It burned in the trees on the church's front lawn and then arrived at the church picket fence. After licking up the grass under the propane tank, it jumped to the back of the parsonage and burned up the pastor's office, consuming his lifelong collection of books and devouring the watercolor paintings from his artistic great-uncle. It burned the log cabin belonging to his resident uncle, as well as the wooden bowls and candlesticks he had carved.

When the fire was gone, all that was left of the outbuildings were rows of nails, which dropped in straight lines from the wooden walls.

Mike Gibbons threaded his way back home through a series of back roads not yet blocked by emergency officials. His son and daughter-in-law came with him. They brought a trailer to the house and loaded it with belongings just in case. If the fire came too close, Mike's daughter-in-law would drive the truck and trailer away, and Mike and his son would stay.

They knew that the time was coming. Smoke swirled in on the wind, wrapping heavy tendrils around the little lot. Explosions echoed. The odor of burning wood scorched their nostrils. Ashes fell.

Mike felt that his firefighting experiences would enable him to meet the challenges ahead. If things got rough, they could move over to his mother's house next door. Her house had much more defensible space around it, set in the middle of a yard, without trees hanging over it like Mike's house. Twenty thousand gallons of water were tanked nearby, pumped by Mike's windmill. With these backup options, Mike was certain they would be safe. There was no way he was going to leave his property and his private museum, Itsatown, to the mercy of the flames.

Mike and his son drove around the neighborhood, watching. They kept an ear to the news and an eye to the sky, where they could see billowing smoke and fire. The fire torched some trees instantly, but others it burned slowly. They watched trees burning around the bottom. Later, they heard the trees crashing to the forest floor.

Bluebonnet Equine Rescue drove up, collecting animals, and Mike sent away his horses and cats and four dogs: a Rottweiler, a Chihuahua, a German shepherd, and a collie.

Mike and his son opened the gate to their pasture of longhorns, giving the animals an option to escape if they needed it.

In the meantime, Shirley had arrived back in Bastrop and had driven straight to her workplace at the *Bastrop Advertiser*, for lack of a better place to go. Officials were not allowing anyone back into the burn zone.

Shirley had finally been able to reach Mike. "Get out now!" she told him. "It's just stuff!"

Of course, Mike tried to convince her that everything was fine.

Suddenly he broke off his conversation with her. Shirley heard him yelling to their daughter-in-law, Morgan. "Get out now!" he was telling her.

As Morgan pulled away with the truck, the fire crossed the road onto Mike's property.

Rather than rushing out to meet the fire approaching through the brush, Mike and his son waited for it to creep into the pasture. In the pasture, where the fuel was mostly short grass, Mike knew they could fight the flames. He shouted directions to his son as they faced the approaching blaze, armed with garden hoses and shovels.

They fought back against the blaze successfully. Not far away, the fire torched the tallest pine trees, the flames rising one hundred feet high. It ignited flammable objects inside neighbors' houses by pouring radiant heat through the window glass. In some houses, the fire melted curtains and drapes, but the houses themselves stood strong.

The fire moved toward the dog kennels at a neighbor's house across the street. It melted open the plastic igloo shapes of some of the kennels, left some of them whole, and completely destroyed others. The fire killed five of the man's dogs, but many more survived with minor burns. Dogs even survived in the kennels that had been melted open.

The fire moved through the woods where two dogs were chained to a tree. One dog managed to struggle free and escape. The other one could not, but somehow he survived as well.

Then the fire moved closer to Mike's house and caught in the neighbor's tall grass. Mike jumped onto his John Deere riding lawn mower and began to mow away the fuel.

The front lawn was carpeted with pine needles. Mike and his son soaked the lawn with water, but Mike knew that even with that protection, it was possible for the fire to creep beneath the needle carpet and stay alive.

Finally, after fighting for several hours, Mike and his son noticed that the fire was not as intense, and it wasn't popping up continually in new places. The wind was pushing it on in search of new fuel.

In the meantime, Morgan drove away with the trailer of animals and possessions. She parked in a place that looked safe beside Highway 21. The firefighters didn't exactly approve of her presence, but there she was. In fact, the emergency officials began to look at her trailer with interest. Finally they came up and asked her if she would be willing to take a few more animals with her out of the burn zone and into town for safe-keeping until they could be reunited with their owners. In this way Morgan formed part of the public rescue effort, driving away with more animals than she had at the beginning of her journey.

Morgan and Shirley met at the Holiday Inn in Bastrop. There they talked and cried. Their husbands were determined to stay in the burn zone regardless of the danger.

They finally reached a decision. "We're going to be in it together," they decided. If their men weren't leaving, they were going to drive back and be with them.

By now the police had blocked off the main back roads as well. Late Monday night, Morgan and Shirley traveled far to the north and began a circuitous route through a series of obscure back roads that even the police had not yet found. They started out around midnight. The fire glowed around them, and they almost got lost in their own backyard.

But they finally made it back.

That night they took turns being on fire watch. Although Shirley had slept Saturday night, the others had not slept well since Friday night. Despite their exhausted state, it was not safe for everyone to fall asleep. The fire could spring up from any side, or it could drop from above.

"Nights were really eerie," Shirley said. "At least you could see the flames. It was *really* dark [because the electricity was out]. You could hear the trees, popping, cracking, falling."

At 4:00 a.m., Mike and his wife—who were supposed to be on fire watch—woke up. They jumped up and looked out to find that the fire had crept onto their property by traveling up the fence line. Together they hurried out to fight it off.

The heat was extreme that night as they tried to unspool the garden hose far enough to reach the blaze. Their garden hose and the soles of their shoes began to melt. But with hand implements and some water from the hose, they fought the fire off.

On Monday, Labor Day, Wesley and Margaret's son looked at an aerial photo of his parents' property and thought the house was still standing. But later the fire changed and headed toward the state park. It began to dance in the trees around Wesley and Margaret's house. Flickering shadows flamed across the bottle house. The fire crept into Wesley's greenhouse and into the chicken house where the hens were just beginning to lay eggs. It burned the wood inside the bottle house gazebo and knocked over the mortared walls full of ten thousand green glass bottles.

The fire burned the front of the house, eating the red paint off Margaret's tricycle as it lunched on the frame of the house. Then it loosened the native stone exterior at the front of the house, causing it to slide to the ground as one piece, as if it were now a sidewalk.

The fire burned the four fire doors. It moved into the antique room. Margaret's spinning wheel, which had survived 160 tumultuous years of

American history, now popped and crackled, finally consumed by a Texas forest fire. The flames burned the quilt from Margaret's grandmother and the trunk from her mother.

Without even the cooling influence of a fireman's hose, the fire burned hot and completely. It burned through the 21-foot built-in shelves and cupboards. Souvenirs from Honduras and rice china from Panama fell to the burning carpet.

Only the fireplace stood strong and did not fall as the house burned around it and the roof fell in.

It had taken Wesley seven years of Saturdays to build the house from local wood, native stone, fabric-padded walls, and stalactites and stalagmites from a nearby cave.

The fire destroyed it in just a few hours.

The next thing Margaret saw of their house was a photo taken by a friend. Only a piece of garage wall, part of the foundation, and the fireplace were left standing. The roof was gone. The large deck was gone. The four fire doors were gone. Nothing that documented their life history was left except the fireproof box, the few other things they had grabbed, and the photos in the safe deposit box at the bank.

The fire burned Nicholas Cowey's four thousand books. It burned his collection of old hymnals and stacks of *National Geographic* magazines.

The fire did not discriminate. It burned the new and inexpensive books and the old and valuable books. It burned the four hundred books from past centuries. It burned the 250 original hand-painted maps from before the time of Lewis and Clark. It burned the book with the fold-out maps of Saxon Germany from 1710, priced at $12,000.

The fire tore through Nicholas's cases of butterflies and lichen specimens. Coonskin caps and 350 animal furs went up in flame along with dozens of other historical costumes.

The inferno melted the window glass, which dripped like icicles. It destroyed the Coweys' sixty-two-piece collection of cast iron. The 1890 reed organ with the seven-foot carved back disintegrated in a roaring crescendo.

The German family of porcelain Hummel figurines on the back of the reed organ fell to the ground, but they did not melt. One of the German figurines chipped his foot, but the family of ten porcelain people remained untouched as the fire roared around them.

Nicholas's worst moment was when a friend texted him to break the news. "Sorry, it's all gone." The house with all its contents. Two cars. And his much-loved dog, Ranger, who died inside the log cabin Nicholas had built for him.

Around Efrain and Debi's log cabin, the fire lit up the brush and the trees that stretched from road to road. The log cabin began to burn. The fire flared high above the logs like a much-too-large campfire. It heated the inside of the log cabin to a tremendous heat. The fire melted the side-by-side refrigerator and freezer into a small pile. The toilet vanished.

The fire consumed family possessions. The family Bible thought to be safest at Debi's house went up in smoke. Family photo albums burned. Efrain's one sample of his father's handwriting was gone in seconds.

Nearby was the house of the neighbor who had called Efrain and Debi and asked, "Should I leave?" Efrain had answered a definite affirmative, which was good advice. Radiant heat reached through the window glass of the neighbor's house, melting the Venetian blinds like wax. But that house did not burn.

The fire burned Alan Donaldson's house on that first night as the world glowed orange in the darkness. It burned his bookcases of books, including Euclid's geometry from 1649. The stamp that said the book was a twin to the Vatican copy went up in smoke. It burned his thirty-five-piece gun collection. It burned the restaurant book he was reading, the home book he was reading, and his phone charger.

At least Alan did not sit in suspense. He knew from the first night that his house and all his possessions were gone.

After trying to sneak back on Highway 21 and being turned back by officials, Bill Ludwig did not give up. He drove back in again and discovered that their house was still standing. Even the outbuildings were safe. But the fire was not over.

After Bill left, the fire came back. It burned the shed full of hobby items and collectibles. It lunched on the four antique pedal cars Bill and Patsy were saving for their grandchildren.

The fire caught in the 370 tall trees, leaping from tree to tree. Fire fell from the trees, dropping burning globs on the grass. Smoke filled the entire clearing. Black soot forced its way into the house, coating every wall and duct. The fine black mist settled on dishes, pictures, pillows, and laundry. Smoke swirled through the air.

The fire stepped through the grass, crawling closer and closer to Bill and Patsy's house. The orange flame, glowing in the smoke, melted the skirting of the house and outbuildings. It crawled under the large propane tank beside the house.

But the house stood strong.

The fire burned through Larry Miller's farm, torching his nine outbuildings and his forty-year collection of tools and mounted animals. It ate up his mounted sailfish and the special feed he had bought for his goats. The fire transformed his riverboat into a pool of aluminum covered with ash and smoke. Flames crawled into the rubber of tractor tires and burned every flammable tractor off its skeleton of metal.

The fire chased Larry's expensive goats through the pasture, choking them with heavy gray smoke. Blindly, the goats ran through the cut wires. They climbed the steps of Larry's house, taking cover under the porch. The house did not burn.

Larry had been working on the trains when the fire started, and he didn't know what was happening. Later he admitted he was glad he wasn't there, because he knows he likely would have been killed retrieving valuables such as his lifelong collection of tools.

As the fire burned down Tall Forest Drive, it burned the tall trees that gave Jimmy Mack's property a resort quality.

It was 7:15 p.m. when the firefighters on Tall Forest Drive radioed a message.

"Looks like the fire is running down Tall Forest. We have multiple structures on fire. We are driving out between two walls of fire. All units evacuate—evacuate! Let's get off Tall Forest. Just keep your eyes on the side of the road and work your way out of here."

The fire burned Jimmy's house. It burned open the waterbed under which the cat had been hiding. It burned the mop Jimmy had used to poke the cat out from under the bed. It burned the kitchen island where they had caught the cat, leaving only the metal drawer sliders.

Flames rifled through office papers and found their passports. It burned up the passport stamps from Egypt, China, Nepal, India, and Cambodia.

Jimmy was sitting at a table at Maxine's Labor Day morning when someone told him that his house was gone. As he absorbed the news, he was in good company. His friend Tommy Hoover, the restorer of old houses, had lost his remodeled village. None of it came as a shock now, even though twenty-four hours before, the thought hadn't crossed Jimmy's mind.

By Monday afternoon many federal resources had arrived to fight the Bastrop fire. These firefighters were the best in the world, having much experience fighting wildfires. They were especially familiar with fires in the mountains and the huge western forests of California. They often protected houses as well, but they were not accustomed to situations in which so many houses and trees clustered in one place.

George Martinez was asked to be the guide for one of the non-local commanders in charge of the area south of Highway 71 near George's home in Tahitian Village. By Monday night, there were more than eighty fires in that area alone. It was the commander's job to supervise the firefighters as they fought these fires and created and defended fire boundary lines.

The commander was experienced in fighting wildfires across the nation, but he always requested to have a local person with him to direct. George, knowing all the back roads, became the commander's GPS. The two drove around for the first few hours that night, assigning tasks and checking on the crews battling the many blazes.

Even with eighty fires, the situation was beginning to look more manageable. It seemed as though the wind was finally dying down. More resources were on the way. They felt that the tide was about to turn. Most of the houses in Tahitian Village were still standing strong.

George looked across Tahitian Drive at a Spanish-style house. It had defensible space, with no trees or shrubs leaning against it. It had stucco walls, a metal roof, and even a wall around it. It looked impenetrable. He was glad when he saw houses like this, because he knew they were not likely to burn.

George and the commander were in their truck close to Tahitian Drive when the wind picked up again. It blew from the north and a huge blaze exploded over Bastrop State Park, just north of Tahitian Village across Highway 71.

"We're losing it, George, we're losing it!" the commander exclaimed, stunned. With all his experience in California and around the nation, he had never seen a scenario quite like this one. With the tightly packed trees and houses, it was a fire plain of unusual proportions.

Both men knew what would happen next.

The mammoth blaze reached hundreds of feet into the air. Then the rain of fire began on the village. "It was like Sodom and Gomorrah," George Martinez recalled.

The fire came down and leaped across Tahitian Drive, burning low in the underbrush before leaping up to blow high in the trees. Burning embers rained down on the roofs of the homes in the subdivision.

In minutes, eighty houses were blazing.

George watched in disbelief as a burning ember dropped onto the Spanish-style house with stucco walls, a metal roof, an impenetrable wall, and defensible space. He hadn't noticed the one wooden beam that was sticking through the stucco wall. The ember started the beam on fire. It followed the beam into the house, and soon the unburnable house was ablaze.

Similar situations were happening all over Tahitian Village. In addition, a silent fire crept up in the grass, through the ravines and over the hills. It crept along wooden fence lines. The fire followed the grass or the fence until it reached a house, finally jumping onto wooden decks or blazing up into the eaves.

The firefighters continued throwing fuel away from the houses. They opened gates, breaking the line of fire. One Tahitian Village homeowner made the firefighters' job easier by turning on his lawn sprinklers before leaving. All the neighboring houses burned, but his stayed strong.

This was George Martinez's home area. He knew the people who lived in these houses. His neighbors. His pastor. He wanted to call all resources to a house and say, "Everyone stop and come over to this house—this is the pastor's house!" But there was no way to concentrate all the help in one place. The firefighters could not get to every house at once.

George didn't know if his house was still standing or not, but he released it to God. "Thank you, Lord, it's been a great house," he prayed.

George learned a lot from the commander that night. First, the commander checked to make sure that all his crews were still safe. He got in touch with each one. When this was verified, they tried to regain their foothold on the fire. They had to readjust their fire lines because the fire had not stayed within the boundaries they had determined.

When Ryan awoke that Monday, he continued to serve the firefighters and answer calls from friends wondering what was happening.

Finally the firefighters insisted that Ryan and his mother leave. Ryan still wasn't afraid that the flames would destroy his apartment, so he just threw a few things together and hurried away in Betsy.

Not many hours later, Ryan heard that the fire was actually quite close to his house. He suddenly remembered important papers and other possessions he might need. Tahitian Drive was of course blocked, but Ryan knew remote ways into the village that few others did.

Ryan had a couple of neighbors who also wanted to slip back in for something. He tried to explain how to get in the back way, but no one could understand his directions. The paths were better suited for motorcycles than cars. So the friends met, and Ryan led the way.

Betsy, the faithful red minivan, crashed down the narrow path, bumping over Tahitian Village's hills. The bumper cracked. A side mirror snapped. The driver's door dented against an obstruction.

Ryan drove into a cul-de-sac, trying to reach a friend's house. Suddenly he realized he was surrounded by flame, with no room to turn. Just then a helicopter thumped overhead, releasing a load of water. It smacked against Betsy, shaking the van, but the nearby flames curled up and died. Ryan opened the door of his friend's house to let the pets escape.

He then drove to his apartment through the swirling smoke. Except for the firefighters, no one was around. Stray cats and dogs milled about. The fire was close, the air thick with smoke. Ryan ran into the house and started throwing a few things together. *Why am I sweating?* he wondered. He looked at the wall thermometer—130 degrees. Outside his window, the dumpster across the alley was burning.

He hurried outside. A firefighter yelled at him, wondering why he was there. He tried to start Betsy, but the smoke was so thick it stalled the van. Jerking the van into neutral, he pushed it down the driveway. Explosions boomed around him.

Betsy started up in the new location, and Ryan gratefully drove away. However, he hadn't gone far when the van stalled again. This time, he waited until a breath of wind blew away the smoke, giving his van more oxygen. Betsy started up again, and Ryan finally left the subdivision as he had been told to do.

FIGHTING FIRE FROM THE AIR

Large forest fires are fought with various kinds of aircraft. Helicopters bring containers of water that weigh up to twenty-one thousand pounds. Airplanes drop a special retardant onto the fire. The ingredients in the fire retardant include fertilizer salts, water, flow conditioners, and red food coloring. The fertilizer salts help destroyed wood to decompose more quickly and also hinder ignition. The food coloring makes the splashes visible, enabling the crew to see the area on which the retardant lands.

On Sunday, the first day of the Bastrop fire, there were three aircraft and three drops, totaling 2,250 gallons of retardant. The next day there were 21 aircraft and 485 drops, for a total of 539,986 gallons. On Tuesday there were 522 drops. The number of drops then decreased the rest of the week. In all, the aircraft dropped 2,059,323 gallons on the Bastrop area in the first week at a cost of $794,441.04.[3] This sounds like a big number, but it is about 0.4 percent of the total estimated loss sustained in the fire, which was more than $209 million.

12

BANDING TOGETHER

Down at the Bastrop Convention Center, now the center of the EOC, Mike Fisher and Judge McDonald worked hard to keep the people of Bastrop informed of what was going on in the fire zone. The EOC became the home base for news reporters, utility crews, insurance adjusters, volunteers, and civilians. Once information began to trickle in, Mike posted lists of the destroyed homes. Each day he updated them as new information rolled in and hundreds of buildings had to be added to the list. Haggard civilians rushed up to the taped papers and stood frozen before them as their eyes rapidly scanned the addresses listed on the charts, hoping they would not see their own.

Two deaths had been reported early in the fire. The bodies were identified as a 58-year-old woman and a 48-year-old man from different areas of the fire zone. The man had been employed by the city of Austin as a master electrician. Little was known about the woman beyond the driver's license photo that was finally released, and the assumption that she had died of smoke inhalation. With deference to family and friends, officials kept the stories surrounding their deaths away from the public eye.

On Monday, the second day of the fire, the EOC sent out cadaver dogs and people experienced in finding bodies. Mr. Fisher and Judge McDonald were afraid that with the massive size of the fire, the dogs would find many bodies. For the first time since the fires started, the news was better than expected.

"We don't know why, but we're not finding bodies. They're just not there," the search teams reported. Judge McDonald and Mike Fisher felt a wave of relief upon realizing they would not need the refrigerated trucks and body bags that had been ordered.

Mr. Fisher and Judge McDonald spoke to the crowd from behind a podium labeled with the seal of the state of Texas. They stood back against the brick façade of the convention center, speaking into a forest of microphones.

Residents became frustrated because of restrictions on returning to their homes. People had two questions for the judge. "Is my house gone?" and "When can I get back in?" Everyone knew that hundreds of homes had been burned. The homeowners wanted to know the truth even if their houses had been decimated.

Their urgency was well-founded. Unless they were planning to leave the area, the market for rental housing was instantly competitive. Those who found out immediately that their house was destroyed had first chance to find a new place to stay.

Mike Fisher tirelessly updated the lists taped to the glass in front of the EOC, adding new information as soon as it became available.

Judge McDonald reminded people of the hidden concerns, such as the burning holes in the ground that no one could see. There were pockets of fire and hundreds of trees about to fall. Electric lines were down, and the roads were impassable.

Not all of these dangers were visible. Soon after the fire, pine needles that weren't burned fell from dying trees and carpeted the burned and scarred areas. They touched the black, smoking land with a healing caress, but they hid burning root holes. Sometimes the fire would burn down a root for days and then pop out of the ground in a different place.

The general manager of Bluebonnet Electric Cooperative also spoke to the public. First of all, he told civilians it would be useless to call the power company and tell them the power was out because, of course, they already knew that. He also cautioned them about touching electric lines. One man had been seen walking into a restricted area and picking up a downed power line.

"We assumed that power line was de-energized, but that's not the way to find out," the general manager said, drawing laughter from the tense crowd.

Bluebonnet Electric posted a full-page ad in the *Bastrop Advertiser*. "Our crews have been working nonstop to make the area safe and restore your power," the ad promised. It invited readers to follow their wildfire restoration work on Twitter or Facebook.[1]

Lieutenant Governor David Dewhurst claimed that President Obama was delaying a disaster declaration because of hard feelings against Rick Perry, the Texas governor who had just joined the presidential race.[2]

Mike Fisher, on the other hand, watched the request for assistance move from Judge McDonald to Governor Perry to President Obama, and felt that the whole process was lightning fast. Regardless of opinions, the Federal Emergency Management Agency (FEMA) personnel on the ground in Bastrop pushed as hard as they could to get a disaster declared for the fire so that aid could come more quickly. They were in Bastrop anticipating the declaration well before it was made.

The Texas Forest Service staff arrived. Gayle, the judge's secretary, was grateful for their assistance with updating the media. The service had staff who worked as full-time public information officers, and their experience was invaluable to Gayle.

The judge continued to talk to the community.

"If we were tired, so was he," Gayle said. But the judge insisted on having three press conferences a day to keep the people as up to date as possible. He took questions from civilians during these press conferences, even though emotions in the public were running high.

At its peak, the EOC housed 165 workers. Laptops and plastic totes full of files sprang up at tables amid a litter of snack bars, water, and Gatorade.

"We didn't *eat lunch,*" Gayle says. "If we were eating, we were checking our email or answering the phone or answering questions."

It was far from the calm privacy of Gayle's office with the maroon leather chairs and the serene hanging plants.

Gayle remembers feeling ineffective because she worked continually without feeling as though she were accomplishing anything. At the same time, she noticed a bond forming between the people working together. People who had been friends before became better friends. She herself found common ground with those whom she had never seen a reason to interact with before. Perspective changed when co-workers were experiencing similar losses.

Gayle and the other public officials had to disconnect themselves personally to keep on going. Gayle was not able to eat supper with her family for many nights. At one point her own home was in danger. At another point she knew her son was helping with animals down at the sale barn, and she heard the fire was heading his direction. Through all this, she had to continue her job.

Every day at the press conference, Gayle would look out over the sea of faces and see another face that she knew—someone who had lost his home or was in some way personally affected by the fire. When her best friend had to evacuate, Gayle simply could not talk to her. It would have been too emotional. For the time, emotions had to wait.

On the thirteenth day after the fire, Gayle's emotions broke when she took a phone call from a dear friend. She burst into tears, terrifying her friend, who had never seen Gayle crack emotionally.

Someone in the EOC from out of town pulled Gayle aside. "We wondered when it would happen," the worker said comfortingly. "It always does."

Judge McDonald identified with the stress of the situation. "We didn't get rest during that time," he explained.

But even without rest, the judge realized there was something special about the responses of people after the fire. He began to wish he could bottle the kindness and hold onto it. Even though it was the biggest incident in Texas during his thirteen years in office, he felt that something beautiful would come from the fires.

"Sometimes we're deceived into thinking we can stand alone," the judge said. The Bastrop fire proved otherwise.

Once again, in the spirit of the past, Maxine's became the fire ring around which hard-pressed citizens could gather. It was the place to be reassured that a new normal would eventually come about. There was at least one place on earth that had not changed; it was still frying up pancakes a foot wide with blueberries that had been dropped into the batter one by one. Wesley Peschke could still order his vegetable platter with the sweet potato in praline sauce. Jimmy Mack, Tommy Hoover, and their comrades could still drink their coffee and discuss the world away from the smell of smoke and the sight of an eastern sky murky with the side effects of fire. In short, the world had not totally fallen apart as long as there were still wide wedges of pie in Maxine's cooler.

Was the Bastrop Complex Fire anyone's fault? This question slipped into every fire discussion around every table at Maxine's. Perhaps Bluebonnet Electric had not trimmed the trees back far enough from the power lines. Perhaps if they had done a better job, the falling tree that hit the power lines would have fallen harmlessly.

But many people didn't feel it was fair to blame Bluebonnet. They were convinced there would have been no human way to prevent the Bastrop Complex Fire.

Firefighters were well cared for at Maxine's. Everyone appreciated their effort, especially on that first long night when they had fought the fire alone. When Alan Donaldson came to Maxine's for his usual breakfast, he was not allowed to pay for it. "Firefighters couldn't pay for a meal for about a month," he said.

The mood over biscuits and gravy at Maxine's wasn't exactly sad. It was just different. One diner asked her waitress if she had been affected by the fire. The waitress admitted she had lost her home. The diner left a hundred-dollar tip.

13

PETS IN THE INFERNO

Troy Walters of Bastrop County Animal Shelter pointed out that the pet owners in Bastrop County were more laid back than the ones in the city of Austin. In Austin, a family might have one pet, carefully vaccinated, medicated, neutered, and taken on routine vet visits. In Bastrop County many people lived on farms or ranches. Rather than owning lap dogs or one specialty cat, these residents wanted big dogs. They might own five or more dogs, with or without rabies shots. The large white Pyrenees was a popular ranch dog. If ranches had a couple of extra acres, they would buy a horse or some sheep. Then they would often buy a donkey to keep predators away from their sheep or goats.

Some people were able to take their animals with them when they evacuated from the fire. Some animals were turned loose by emergency personnel, giving them the freedom to escape if they could.

In the aftermath of the fire, the burn scar was filled with lost pets, searching for homes that no longer existed. With them, wild animals wandered, looking for food that no longer existed.

Stray animals were taken to Troy Walters at the Bastrop County

Animal Shelter, a white block building surrounded with white gravel, a cactus, and a chain-link fence. Although it sat northeast of the fire scar, it was close enough that the shelter itself had been forced to evacuate for a time.

The animal shelter was deluged with animals needing a place to stay. Post-disaster motels kindly accepted pets, so many owners were able to keep their pets with them. However, many animals were wandering free and got picked up by people and brought to the animal shelter. If they were injured, they were sent to Austin or cared for by veterinarians.

The September census at the animal shelter jumped from 130 to 500.

"The animals were traumatized," Mr. Walters said. Cats were wide-eyed, covered with ash and smelling like smoke. Dogs acted depressed, lying listlessly in their kennels, totally anti-social. Many animals had injuries, and many had to be humanely euthanized. Some could be nursed back to health with care.

Mr. Walters noted that one reason so many animals were homeless was that many families had gone on trips over the Labor Day holidays, leaving their animals at home. Mr. Walters himself had been away, although he had taken his dogs with him, as always.

People came to the animal shelter every day, hoping to find their lost pets. As they sat in the lobby of the shelter, awaiting their turn, poster-sized glossy photos of napping pets stared down at them. Lost and found and wanted posters were taped to the block walls of the waiting area.

Even though Mr. Walters had his own pets, he still enjoyed walking into the long buildings with the rows of dog kennels or into the cat room. He especially loved taking families into the buildings to search for their lost pets.

If the right owner returned for a dog, a transformation happened. When the dog heard the owner's voice, it would sit up. When it saw its owner, its tail would start wagging. The old, depressed visage would fall off like a shell, and the dog would jump and frolic.

The animal shelter provided refuge to more than dogs and cats. One day Mr. Walters got a call from the fire department. They were working in a burned area and being followed by a large tortoise. Besides the eeriness of being shadowed by such a creature, they thought their new follower should have a home.

"It was as big around as your arms," said Mr. Walters, forming a large circle with his arms.

Mr. Walters collected it and called an expert from the Central Texas Zoo.

"What kind is it?" the expert asked.

"I don't know; it's a big one," said Mr. Walters.

"Is it male or female?" was his next question.

"I don't know . . . it's a big turtle."

The expert from the zoo came to see for himself.

"Oh, it's an African spur," he said, identifying the breed well known for its pleasant temperament. Flipping it over, he noted that it was a female.

Even though the animal shelter was overflowing, Mr. Walters found a temporary corner for the tortoise. Since large tortoises were not native to Bastrop, he thought someone might come looking for it.

One evening, after the animal shelter was closed for the night, they heard someone outside the closed gate and went to investigate.

"I just want to know if anyone found a tortoise," the person said. And so the tortoise was reunited with her owner.

Another day a family came looking for a white rat named Cheeto. They also had turtles and a dog at their home, but they had already found the dog at a shelter, and they knew the turtles had died in the fire. Their neighbor had called them when they were fleeing to say that their bedroom was on fire, and later they found that their house had burned to the ground. They thought maybe Cheeto, the white rat, had escaped.

Cheeto was a family favorite. Not only that, he had a history of escape.

"He's such an escape artist," the family said. In happier times, Cheeto would slip out of his cage at night, flatten himself under their bedroom doors, and crawl into bed with them. Knowing that Cheeto had these skills, they thought it was possible that he had not gone up in smoke with the house.

As a matter of fact, the animal shelter told them, the firefighters had brought in a white rat. With great delight, the family was reunited with Cheeto. He had passed the ultimate test, escaping from a forest fire. The firefighters had brought him to the shelter, whole and unharmed, his white coat glistening and his nose still pink.

It didn't happen often, but occasionally there was an argument about which family an animal belonged to. Once, a family collected a cat, saying they were sure it was theirs. Later, another family came, inquiring about a cat with the same description. They said they had embedded a microchip in the cat, which proved to be correct. The cat was returned to the correct owners.

ANONYMOUS ANIMAL STORIES

Some people retrieved their animals but had no good place to keep them. Vehicles became over-stuffed kennels. One lady kept her animals in her car: ten dogs, seven cats, ferrets, guinea pigs, and fish. Another person kept a 100-pound pot-bellied pig in a car.

One couple had eighty cats. They tried to get them out of their house, but the task was simply too great. Finally the deputy who had come to warn them said, "If I tell you a third time, I'm putting the handcuffs on you." They left with about half of their cats.

Another lady had twenty-two animals at her house. When the fire got close, she loaded three milk goats, ten chickens, a giant carnivorous lizard, a songbird, and a whippet into her truck. She towed her two stallions beside the truck, holding onto their ropes through the truck window as she drove away. The lady did not report how the carnivorous lizard got along with the chickens in the back. She took them to a friend's ranch and then turned back to get the birds she had not been able to bring along.

She was able to retrieve the birds, but she also began to realize how serious the fire was. When she arrived back at her friend's ranch, she noticed that it was also in danger. They fought with water out of the horse troughs until it became unmanageable and ineffective. The friend's stucco house went up in smoke, probably from a burning ember landing in the eaves. The couple described "tornadoes of fire" around them as they finally retreated into a pickup truck and waited out the fire there. The friend's barn also burned, and with it the three milking goats that had just been secured there. Her horses survived, but their tails got singed.

Word began to circulate that chickens have a natural defense against fire. They turn their backs to the fire and claw at the sand, creating a fine shower of sand to smother the approaching blaze. If their tails catch on fire, chickens reportedly retreat, where they stop, drop, and roll before dashing back to fight the blaze again with their backs turned and their feet flying.

14

GOING ON IN FAITH

It took four weeks to put out the last flame and many more weeks to sort through the ruin.

Like a campfire, the forest fire smoldered on after the flames were gone. Some areas were black, and some, like the top of campfire logs, were white with ash. The firefighters worked through the blackened landscape, looking for hidden pockets of fire smoldering in stump or root holes. To search for heat, they reached their bare hands into the holes. The human hand was the easiest, most reliable test. When they did find fire or hot spots, they soaked the areas with water from their hoses.

The firefighters worked on a landscape that oozed smoke particles and smelled like charcoal. They worked beside dozens of trees waiting to fall. Some of the trees were carved into bizarre shapes like a totem pole, where the wind had driven the fire deep into the heart of the tree. Others were blackened only on the downwind side where the oils from the tree had collected, creating a pipeline to the treetop.

The firefighters worked in a dangerous emotional landscape as well. They knew that, with the greatest danger past, civilians were frustrated, hurting, and angry. The media was pulling out, reality was setting in, and still the firefighter's work was continuous and essential.

The Texas Forest Service, along with Mike Fisher, picked seven trampolines out of the Bastrop fire scar. These trampolines were an excellent record of the fire, because although they were still intact, they were pockmarked with holes from the burning embers that had fallen on them. The forest service marked the location of each trampoline on a map of the Bastrop fire. Then they studied the trampolines to see which areas of the fire had been most intense. From this study, they were able to make conclusions about the direction of the wind. They were able to conclude which areas of the fire were the most dangerous, giving them valuable guidelines for the future.[1]

According to Mike Fisher, the firefighting effort peaked around September 12. On that day there were 633 firefighters, 500 electric linemen, 200 law enforcement officers, and 200 water and waste utility workers to be fed and coordinated. The firefighters came from every corner of Texas and nineteen other states. There were vehicles to be fueled, cars to be rented, equipment to be repaired, flat tires to be fixed, and burned hose to be replaced. Thankfully, amid a rash of blisters and Band-Aids, there were only two serious medical injuries to firefighters.

AFTER THE FLAMES ARE GONE

Even after the flames are gone, a forest fire is not over. The fire continues to burn the wood, although if the tree is alive and well-hydrated, this will probably not last long. Sometimes the white ash, which is all that is left of the wood, will collapse on the remaining fuel and smother the fire. This is why rearranging a campfire enables the fire to burn longer, because it shakes off the ash and keeps it from smothering the fire. If a piece of fuel—a pine twig, or one of Nicholas Cowey's four thousand books—burns completely, it may retain its shape for a time. A delicate web of white mineral ash will remain. However, as soon as there is a wind or some disturbance, the shape will collapse and the remains will float away in the breeze.

Wildfires with heavy fuels can produce two or more tons of smoke particles per acre.[2] Smoldering can go on for days, even weeks, in the roots of dead trees, creating dangerous fire holes into which an unsuspecting person might plunge a foot. This is a big reason why evacuations need to last as long as they do.

Perhaps the other biggest danger in a post-fire landscape is the trees that were dead before the fire occurred but are still standing. These trees, with their lower water content, burn much more completely. Their roots may be burned right out from under them, making them extremely susceptible to falling.

Two days after the fire started, Dean and Debra, along with Howard and Holly, made their way to Alum Creek Drive. It looked like a war zone. There was nothing on the ground; everything had been burned. They simply could not recognize their own road, even though the sun was shining down cheerily.

When they pulled into Alum Creek Drive for the first time, Debra had no idea what she would see. The countryside was laid waste, a black skeleton showered with white and marred with twisted metal skeletons. Debra doubted that there could be anything left, either of their house or of the two vehicles they had packed full of school supplies and curriculum.

However, as they drove up Alum Creek Drive, they saw the two vehicles standing untouched at the end of the cul-de-sac. They were still packed full. There was no scratch on the van, and neither vehicle was charred. All around them, ruined homes and charred vehicles lay twisted and useless.

"It wasn't the van that the Lord was saving; it was your work," Dean told Debra. In the van was much of the work she had carefully prepared for her home school and for the One Day Academy where she taught. She had even saved the graded papers the students had handed in to her. How surprised they would be to find out that their papers had survived the fire!

They started up the driveway. The vehicles were on a rise, over which the ground sloped down to the trailer. There were a few other mobile homes left in the little court. Perhaps their neighbor had been wrong and theirs was okay!

But as they drove over the rise, the only thing to meet their eyes was the twisted metal undergirding that had held the trailer together. Everything was black with soot or white with ash. Even the towering pines were black. The fireproof safe and refrigerator were both destroyed. The aluminum had melted in puddles.

But behind the ruin was something green. Just a few yards from the apocalypse, the green plastic pickle swing still dangled from the oak tree by its nylon rope. Amid the scorched pine trees, the oak tree was a little brown, but not black.

Peace filled Debra's heart like water pouring into a glass. The plastic pickle swing had not melted! Her husband's childhood swing, which had become the childhood swing of their children, had stood in the middle of a raging forest fire, only a few yards from the roaring fire of a mobile home, and had not been burned.

Debra heard the Lord whisper to her spirit, "I can save what I want to save. You know I'm sovereign. You also know I'm good. If I wanted the house to be here, it would still be here."

The men decided to trudge through the smoldering woods to where Howard and Holly lived, to see if their home was still there. Debra and Holly sat together by the ruin of Debra's home, waiting for the men to return. From the ground around them, smoke curled and rose. Yet, although surrounded by ruins, the women did not feel like crying. Debra thought of the Bible story where King David's son died. David quit mourning after it was clear there was no more hope of saving him. The Lord had made His choice clear about Dean and Debra's house.

But what had the Lord decided about Howard and Holly's?

"Do you think we can read their faces?" they asked each other, anticipating the men's return through the woods.

When the two men appeared, Debra had no doubt. "Your house is gone, honey. I can see your husband's face," she said.

"I know," Holly acknowledged as the two men walked slowly and quietly back to their wives.

Friends of Debra and Dean offered them a place to stay. The children stayed with their grandparents in Austin while Dean and Debra ran around making arrangements. So many people were generous. Many organizations were set up at the high school: the IRS, the Red Cross, St. Vincent de Paul. People could come in for gas cards and emergency packs.

Knowing that Jorja had always wanted a pink room, the friends who offered their house allowed Jorja's room to be painted pink with flowers and butterflies. Before the children returned to their temporary home, Dean and Debra spread out the clothes they had received from friends and relief organizations. It was almost like Christmas, a wonderful surprise for the four children whose home had been destroyed.

The host family at the temporary home apologized to the Pahlows about the mismatching carpets, the age of the appliances, and the stain on the ceiling. Debra stared at them.

"This place is a palace," she said. The temporary home had a concrete foundation and central air and heat. You couldn't even know what the weather felt like without going outside.

"This house is better than our old house," the children told Debra.

"I know," she laughed.

A new normal began to develop. The father of one of Debra's students organized a squadron of volunteers who helped with cleanup at the house site. They cleared, cut, blowtorched, shoveled, and hauled the lot clean in less than eight hours.

"Do you want us to sift?" they asked.

"No," the Pahlows said. "But if you happen to find something while you clear, sure, we'd like to see it."

In the ash, a worker found the metal-work cross called the "Eye of the Storm." The cross was damaged but recognizable, and Debra stuck it prominently in a burned-out stump in the front yard.

It seemed like another sign that God was saying, "It's going to be okay."

Dean and Debra's pastor was equipped for action when the fire came. First he looked up all his church members, wanting to know if they were okay. When he found the people, many of them had immediate needs. Not all of them had had time to grab their cell phones before evacuating. Even more people had grabbed their cell phones but not their chargers. Some people had only the clothes on their backs and just needed to go to Walmart to buy basics like underwear and socks and toothpaste.

Thankfully, the pastor had money from the church offering that he was planning to deposit. This time, instead of depositing it, he decided to turn it back to the church family. He put up to two hundred miles on his car some days that week, tracking down the church members and handing out cash for their needs.

Thirty-four families regularly attended the small white church. Half of their homes had been completely burned out. It was a colossal event for the church.

The church and parsonage were still standing, despite the fire that had burned up to their picket fence and licked up the grass under the propane tank. Many of the large trees that had stood in front of the church were destroyed, and the outbuildings were gone.

The pastor returned on Monday, September 12. "It was total devastation," he said. "Everything was black. There was no grass. Nothing. It looked like a war zone, something like after the Germans bombed the villages in World War II."

The pastor found it to be both amazing and heartbreaking—amazing that so much could be destroyed in so short a time, and so sad to see just piles of rubble left. "I don't know that I've ever been quite so devastated by visual stuff," he said.

There was no time to despair, however. The small white church soon became a main hub of activity. A relief organization, Texas Baptist Men, came with their resources and started a laundry and feeding unit at the small church. There were four showers, three washers, and two dryers. Everyone in the community was welcome. Four or five people set up tents in the blackened front yard of the church.

The church ladies assisted by setting up the church kitchen and delving into the pantry of stockpiled goods the pastor had laid away for such a time as this. Space was limited, but they set up tables in the church and served three meals a day for about six weeks. Other tables at the church were piled with clothes, towels, diapers, and hygiene products available for the needs of the fire victims.

As the ladies worked in the kitchen, the pastor rented a bulldozer and offered his services to whoever needed bulldozer work. Because the church went out and helped the people at no charge, they had a lot of opportunities to share the Gospel with those who otherwise would have had no interest.

The testimonies of those who had experienced many losses themselves were especially powerful. One of their own church members who had lost his home and business was one of the most dedicated volunteers, taking the bulldozer to different places. "He never missed a day," the pastor's wife remembers.

But everyone reacted differently. One man moved to Austin and took out a fifteen-month lease on an apartment. When asked if he was planning to come back, he answered, "I don't want to get burned up in a fire."

The pastor's wife felt that it was hard for him to look at the situation objectively. The Bastrop fire had been the only major fire in years. Austin had small fires all the time. But still he felt safer there than in the place that he had actually seen go up in flames.

"I know what's kept me going," the pastor's wife said, "and it's been the Lord. He's given me the strength and determination to keep going. And everybody's situation is different. You look and you think you know what to do, but you don't really. The book of James tells us we're going to have trials and we should give thanks."

Could Debra go back to teaching homeschooled students at the One Day Academy? Her director told her that it was okay if she couldn't. At the same time, he felt that the students—especially those who had lost their houses—would look to Debra for an example of how to respond. If Mrs. Pahlow withdrew for a month, it could affect her students negatively.

The One Day Academy at Bastrop Christian Outreach Center was cancelled for the first week after the fire, since it had become a fire shelter. However, almost as soon as the doors were open, Debra was back.

When she walked into her classroom, relief flooded her. "This is normal!" she said. A sense of normality brought relief after all the upheaval since the fire. Several of her students empathized with her; they had also lost their homes.

But a student who had not lost his home said lightly, "Normal is overrated."

"No, it's not," Debra corrected him quickly. "You say that kind of flippantly, and it's kind of cute. But did you sleep in your own bed last night? Did you have a computer to do your homework on? Did you have a printer to print your papers?"

Debra had several encounters with people who thought she should be cynical.

Outside the white block walls of the Bastrop Library, someone had posted a fire damage map. Debra was looking at this map when a woman standing beside her commented on the enormity of the red-shaded burn area.

"I bet all those Christians who are going around saying 'Praise God' are singing a whole different tune now."

Shocked, all Debra could reply was, "But I am! My house burned to the ground right there." She pointed to the center of the red. "But I'm still praising Him."

Now it was the other woman's turn to be shocked. "Really?"

"Yeah."

The woman couldn't even reply; the words seemed to catch in her throat. Exasperated, she threw up her hands and stalked away without even a polite goodbye.

Debra also shared some thoughts about the disaster on Facebook.

> I am sitting on a stack of cinder blocks behind what used to be our house. Twisted metal, melted glass, the charred remains of my daughter's little day bed surrounded by the sweet chirping of birds and a cool, gentle breeze through the singed pines. Yes, God is still on His throne. His eyes have taken in everything. I am thankful for the time He allowed me to have in this house. I found my Lord out here in these pines. I cannot wait to see what He will teach me next.

Beneath the comments of encouragement and support, a friend of Debra's who did not have faith in God posted a message:

"Ah, yeah, but by the same token, 'He' burned your houses down and you did nothing to deserve that. Reality check, people. At least no one was hurt."

Debra knew she had to reply to this cynical comment, and she had a message to give.

> True, God is sovereign. However, I also recognize that He

is good. I don't view this as a punishment, so I'm not angry. Sad, yes . . . I was feeling quite comfortable as of late . . . These lessons are gained through trial, through fire as it were. But just as fire burns away the slag from silver, so He is refining me as well. Moreover, I trust that He will not leave me in the fire any longer than I have to be.

15

HOMES ALONG HIGHWAY 21

As the fire continued to smolder around them, the Gibbons homestead became the headquarters for the small band in the neighborhood that had not evacuated, about fifteen people in all. The Gibbons family was the most versed in survival. On Tuesday, they set up a kitchen. The electricity was gone, so the food in the freezer would spoil soon. Mike and his wife began barbecuing. Amazingly, they didn't lose water altogether. The water was shut off, but the Gibbons homestead was still receiving low pressure water. Mike suspected it was gravity flow since they were positioned in a low spot.

Shirley got out laundry washtubs and an old hand wringer and invited people to do laundry. Mike baked biscuits on the grill. When word got around that Shirley could make coffee without electricity, the neighborhood flocked in. The news of hot coffee spread as quickly as the wildfire had.

As the food began to spoil in the freezer, all of the neighboring animals benefited. Mike temporarily adopted dogs, cats, chickens, ducks, parrots, and pigs, feeding the animals all week. One neighbor had eight parakeets and seven kinds of parrots. Eventually the county animal shelter came and rescued as many animals as they could.

Mike and Shirley's son was interested in the Chinook helicopters. Wanting a closer view of the machines, he ran close to where one was flying overhead. But just at that moment, the helicopter dropped its water. Hit by only a small part of the deluge, the young man was shocked at its intensity. "It hurt!" he told his family. Besides the force of the water on him, the force of water hitting the burned forest floor caused a fountain of ash.

"Well, son, you wanted to see it, and you got a really close view," Shirley laughed.

Several days into it, the landlocked tribe of fifteen began to run out of supplies. Finally, Mike's son and daughter-in-law took a vehicle and left for supplies. They met their grandmother and gathered the supplies, but they quickly realized that they would never be allowed back in. The ban was for good reason: the woods were extremely dangerous, filled with fire pits, sudden flames, and trees ready to fall. However, the young people would not be deterred. They loaded the supplies in their backpacks and drove down Highway 21 to a place where no emergency personnel were posted. Jumping out of the vehicle, they left it with their grandmother and hiked through the woods on foot.

They called Mike and Shirley to tell them they were coming. When Shirley heard that "the children" were trying to walk through the burning woods, her eyes filled with tears and her heart began to pound. She knew it was not safe, but there was nothing she could do but watch for them at the edge of the forest.

Finally, two figures stepped out of the woods. They were covered with a gray coating, unrecognizable. But they were okay. Shirley was so relieved to see them that she didn't care a bit about the soot and ash.

When Shirley made it back to work at the *Bastrop Advertiser*, business was crazy. People swarmed the offices. Some people were very giving; some were very angry. The people who wanted to place an ad made her feel impatient. She realized that some of them truly wanted to help, but many just wanted to make money.

Shirley was humbled by the hard experience. She knew that the event pulled the community together. Yet it had impacted her so deeply that she could not bring herself to drive through the neighborhoods that had been burned completely.

On Thursday, September 8, 2011, the first edition of the *Bastrop Advertiser* since the fire went to the press. Beneath the paper's title was the familiar line: "Texas' Oldest Weekly Newspaper Since March 1, 1853." The front-page picture was a familiar-looking Texas pasture dotted with black beef cows and a cluster of outbuildings in the distance. The pasture was bordered with barbed wire fence and scrubby underbrush.

The unfamiliar part was the sky in the photo: there was none. Instead, a two-toned cloud hung above the pasture, cottony gray with patches of egg-yolk orange. Across the top of the photo, the headline ran just one word: "CATASTROPHIC."

No section of the *Bastrop Advertiser* was normal in that edition. In fact, members of the newspaper staff, like Shirley Gibbons, were experiencing their own tragedies. But like the *Advertiser* in the early days when the oxcarts got stranded bringing paper from Houston, the paper was printed anyway.

On the sports page, the headlines announced local football games that had been canceled. A columnist wrote, "At a time like this, sports are insignificant. There are events in our lives that put everything into perspective for us."[1]

In the normal side column of announcements, prepared before the catastrophe, the old life was still present: flu shots and a meeting at the Bastrop Public Library. On September 11 a service of prayer and thanksgiving was scheduled to be held at Bastrop High School in memory of the terrorist attacks ten years previous.

In the *Bastrop Advertiser* editorial, Cindy Wright wrote, "Last Friday, my biggest problem was that I got a scrambled egg and cheese breakfast taco when I had ordered a migas breakfast taco. A lot has changed since then. . . . It's never a good sign to see numerous media trucks gathered in your town."[2]

Christian Aid Ministries (CAM), later to return in force to provide free labor for rebuilding homes, pitched in with food and tools in the immediate aftermath of the fires.

Food was the main preoccupation for the first two weeks. Stan Miller helped set up a kitchen at Celebration Church, near the animal shelter north of Bastrop. The CAM kitchen served three meals a day. The first Friday, the kitchen didn't close until 11:30 p.m. People just kept coming.

"Can't you fix a little something for these folks yet?" the kitchen staff kept hearing. They just couldn't turn hungry people away. Stan found himself sorting through the refrigerator for latecomers and heating food for them in the microwave. He remembers being so tired that he kept hitting the rumble strips on his way back to the place he stayed for the night.

Donations of food were helpful to Stan and the rest, but sometimes it was hard to tell whether a donation should be accepted. On Sunday afternoon a church group donated ten eight-gallon aluminum vats, each half full of rice and beans leftover from their fellowship dinner. Stan and his partners felt the sides of the vats and discovered the mountains of rice and beans were lukewarm. They suspected that they would not be able to use the food, but what could they say to the donors? They asked the donors to leave the food, but in the end they were not able to use it.

Stan also attended Judge McDonald's press conference in town every day to keep abreast of the changes on the scene.

Three weeks later Stan began to make contacts with local homeowners to see if they needed help with cleanup before rebuilding could begin. He talked to Wesley and Margaret Peschke, Adam and Cindy Cruz, Patty Timmons, and Bill and Patsy Ludwig. He arranged crews to help the homeowners clean up their lots.

With Stan directing, the volunteer crews began. It was an extremely dirty job. Even though Stan was more manager than manual laborer, he, too, was filthy by the end of the day.

Some of the homeowners stayed in touch and later made contact with

CAM's house-building program when they wanted to rebuild.

Wesley and Margaret returned to their property. They had already seen pictures of the lone fireplace standing amid the wreckage of their home, so there were no surprises. Still, driving in the lane was very hard. The bottle house lay in pieces, the roof caved in. Their largest tree was charred, along with many smaller ones and Margaret's favorite oak outside the kitchen window.

Disaster response men from CAM arrived to help Wesley and Margaret clean up their property. One of the men found some dishes that had been in storage in the garage and had survived the fire. Margaret found the red tricycle she had displayed on her front porch. It was badly burned and mangled, but Margaret decided to keep it and put it on her new front porch in memory of the fire.

She decided she would not dig much. She felt the Lord speaking to her, saying, "Don't look back." He was telling her that life must go on despite her grief.

Margaret decided to face the fire. A lot of history had burned up. Pieces of history from Margaret's great-grandmother, as well as Wesley's family, were gone. *That's the past,* she decided. She knew many people were much worse off than they. She decided she would not look back.

There were many reasons to look ahead, because there was much work to do and many decisions to be made. Margaret did not know if the pine trees were all dead or not. Some of the trees had green needles on their tops, but as autumn came, they turned brown. The oaks also had some green, but it was quickly eaten by the starving leafcutter ants.

Wesley and Margaret decided to rebuild on their same property despite the charred ghosts of trees and buildings. Before the debris was shoveled away, they took one last picture together on the threshold of their house, standing on the steps surrounded by ash and broken brick. They had dedicated their house in 1985 on their thirtieth anniversary, and now in 2011, they released it back to God.

Margaret remembered the mission trips and the miracles God had performed. She remembered God's faithfulness through the years, in California and at Southwestern Bell Telephone Company. So when she stood in front of the ruined house with the fireplace standing alone, Margaret saw it through the eyes of a woman who had witnessed God's faithfulness over and over again. She knew she could trust that the God who gave Wesley overtime hours after his mission trips would be there again. She knew she could not out-give God.

Margaret decided to give what she could. Even in the ruin, perhaps there was someone they could bless. The Peschkes decided to donate the largest tree on their property. It was charred and needed to come down, but it contained a lot of good wood. They gave it to an organization building homes for people without insurance. In time their wonderful tall tree would become the framework for the home of someone they would probably never meet.

TIPS FOR RETURNING TO A BURNED-OUT HOME SITE

Homeowners should be careful where they walk. They should identify and report all downed electric wires and definitely not touch them! Because of the likelihood of hidden, sharp objects, people should get a tetanus shot if they haven't had one for ten years. They should use caution as they breathe in the fumes from the fire or ash, and wear masks when appropriate. Leaf-blowers and wild sweeping motions will stir up the ash and should not be used. Wetting an area down or cleaning with a damp cloth can settle the dust and ash.

Extreme caution should be used with damaged trees. Homeowners should not agree to a quick sale of a dead tree for lumber. They should wait for an experienced forester to assess the trees.

> **TREE ASSESSMENT TIPS**
>
> If the life-giving portions of a tree—the roots, stem, or crown—have been seriously damaged, the tree will likely die. If there is charred bark greater than 50 percent of stem height on all sides, the tree will likely die. If there are signs of wood-boring beetles on any part of the stem, or if no green needles are present in the crown two months after the fire, the tree is dead or dying.
>
> For the sake of your insurance company, photograph all damage to the trees before attempting to fix or move anything.

Ten days after the fire, Patty Timmons and her husband were allowed to go back. As they drove toward their home from the north, they noticed with relief that they were driving through green countryside. Yes, the fire had started close to their house, but the wind had forced it south, and they lived slightly north of the original flame. They got closer and closer, and the trees were still unburned. Their neighbor's houses were still standing.

They thought of the people staying with them at La Quinta, displaced Bastropians like themselves. Each night they would gather outside and talk. Some whose homes had received only partial damage had begun to go out and clean. They returned every night, hardly recognizable, covered in soot.

As Patty and her husband drove toward their house, they were so glad to see the green trees. They were thankful that they lived just far enough away from the fire to be out of the danger zone.

Then they turned a corner and received a shock. Their house was gone. Set between the homes of their neighbors and friends was a heap of white ash that used to be their house.

It was a terrible blow. They turned around and drove back to the hotel, too angry and confused to talk about the tragedy. What was there to do? How could it be that only their house had burned?

Disasters tend to draw some people closer together and drive others further apart. At the time when they needed each other the most, Patty's husband of twenty-one years decided to leave her. Even though their house was underinsured, he took half of the money. Patty was devastated, yet she knew that the fire was not entirely to blame for her husband's departure. She determined to take her share of responsibility. As time went on, she heard about other marriages crumbling after the stress of the fire.

Patty went back to the heap of ashes to clean up alone. Thankfully, a friend with a tractor offered to help her haul away the rubble. Patty threw the chain around the pieces of rubble, and the friend hauled them away with his tractor. Right at first the ground was still hot in places. Patty felt the heat radiating out of the ground. She heard about people whose tennis shoes melted from working on the hot ground.

By now Patty was staying at a friend's house. Though her hosts assured her that she was welcome, she felt she was in the way. She tried her best not to inconvenience them. When she came back from the house site, she was covered with soot. Even though she had been wearing socks and shoes, her feet were black when she removed the socks. In the entryway of her friend's house, Patty removed her socks and shoes and wrapped them in a towel so she wouldn't spread the sticky black through the house. Even showering didn't automatically remove the soot. It had to be scrubbed off with effort.

One day a church group of volunteers came out and helped her. Patty was encouraged. She could not believe how much work they accomplished in one day.

Paige Webb, a volunteer coordinator, called Patty and found out about the situation. Patty's house was gone. Her husband was gone. She needed a place to live. How could she secure the money to buy or build a house?

"We'll try Plan A, and then we'll try Plan B, and then we'll try Plan C,"

Paige stated encouragingly. Even if they failed repeatedly, Paige was sure that something would work out for Patty. "We'll go to Plan Z," she promised, "and then start over."

Hearing these words of confidence and encouragement gave Patty new hope.

One of the plans on Paige's list was Christian Aid Ministries. Paige connected Patty with Vernon and Mary Ellen Miller of CAM, who helped her plan a new house that would be built with free labor. Patty feels that both Paige and CAM saved her.

Patty didn't usually cry much when bad things happened, but sometimes she cried in relief. One day, after Patty found out that she would be getting a new house built with free labor, she found herself crying at Lowe's. She had been standing in the fixture aisle with a Lowe's employee, trying to pick out a faucet for her new house. The care the employee was showing touched her heart and made her cry. "I'm fine until someone is nice to me," she said. She hoped the manager wouldn't come around and assume the employee was frustrating her.

Patty was grateful for all the ways people were helping her. In turn, she wanted to give back and help others. She decided to volunteer to help Paige with her work. In this way she could help others in the community who had lost everything as well.

The same church group who had helped her clean up "adopted" her and helped her through the process of getting a FEMA trailer. Just applying for a FEMA trailer seemed like a full-time occupation. Finally the trailer arrived, and she was able to move into her own space. Even though it was small, she felt it was a mansion. She was no longer sleeping in someone else's bed.

Finding a place of emotional stability was harder than applying for a FEMA trailer. The whole experience had been a train wreck, and Patty still found herself sorting through the rubble. She found that she did not want to leave her trailer even to go shopping for fear something would happen while she was gone. The memory was too real—flashbacks of the time she left her house and came back to nothing.

The middle school in Bastrop became a shelter and a meeting place for those affected by the fire. Several days after the fire began, Adam and Cindy were at the middle school. Adam joined the crowd of homeowners around the maps which showed the current extent of destruction. Some home lots were colored red and some were colored blue, but Adam did not know what the color key was. He found his own home and saw it was red, but what did that mean? Finally a firefighter standing nearby answered his question.

"All the red means those properties have been destroyed," he said.

Cindy was talking to a family member on the phone when Adam came up to her and nodded his head. Yes, it was all lost. Cindy ended the call, about to break down.

A volunteer came up and saw her tears. "Are you all right?" she asked.

Cindy explained that she just heard her home was gone. As she cried, Cindy was thinking of the things she had not saved. The many pictures. Caps and gowns from the boys' graduations. Her daughter's dress from her sweet sixteen party. Her children's school records. A sentimental tree given to her by her mother. *I have to get myself back to praying,* she told herself. *I have to fight off the enemy's thoughts.*

"You know the governor's here," the volunteer mentioned as they continued to talk.

Cindy didn't reply, but she thought, *Who cares?*

Then she glanced up—eyes still filled with tears, face distraught, hair disheveled—and there was Governor Rick Perry standing above her.

"Are you . . ." He paused. "Did you lose your home?"

"Yes, sir," she choked out. "That's what my husband just found out."

Governor Perry put his hands on hers.

"I thank God for sparing our lives," Cindy said through her tears. "And I thank you for being governor and for what you've done."

The governor moved on, but Cindy realized she was glad for the opportunity to meet him, praise God in front of him, and thank him for his help all in one short conversation.

Then a man in a wheelchair came up to Cindy and shook her hand. "Ma'am," he began, "are you a victim of the fire?"

"Yes, sir," Cindy said. Unaware that she was talking to a famous man, she praised God as she had done when speaking to Governor Perry. About that time she realized who the man was. This was Texas Attorney General Greg Abbott, whose life story also contained tragedy. Shortly after graduating from law school, Mr. Abbott had been struck by a falling tree while jogging, permanently paralyzing him.[3] Meeting the attorney general made Cindy grateful again. She had been able to praise God, through her tears, before two famous men.

Driving up the road to the site of their old home about two and a half weeks later was extremely difficult for Cindy. Although she knew the house was gone—she had been told that there was nothing left but a few bricks—she could not really believe it. But when they drove up the road through a foreign wasteland, there could be no doubt. Adam was driving, and their son who lived in Bastrop was following. When Cindy got out of the vehicle, her son hurried to her side to support her.

Their son had not lost his house. The fire had burned up to his house, consuming several houses along the road. However, it had spared not only his house, but two cedar cabins he owned. It was phenomenal enough that a firefighter from California had commented about it. He said it was rare to see two cabins like that spared in a fire so severe.

But nothing had been spared at Adam and Cindy's house. The property looked as if a bomb had exploded. It was more white than black. Everything had burned completely, leaving only ash with a few broken rocks scattered here and there. It reminded Cindy of what she imagined the moon's surface to look like. As she looked at the destruction, the image that kept recurring in her mind was of Christmastime. How many happy holiday hours had they spent in the house that had vanished?

What if our son had not called us? Cindy wondered, looking at the remains of a home that had become a furnace. *What if the fire had started at night . . . not just for us, but for all these people who lived here?* She started walking around.

"Be careful," Adam said.

They couldn't even tell where their bedroom had been. They retrieved a few ceramic dolls, the only things they could find that had been spared.

She had not stopped praying through the whole experience, but she had quit reading her Bible in all the upheaval. Suddenly she caught herself. *I'm drawing away from God,* she realized.

With time, Cindy's hope returned as she and Adam worked on cleaning through the rubble of what had been their home. Cindy's faith remained strong. She spray-painted encouraging words on the broken rock walls of their house with messages such as, "Thank you, Jesus, for saving all these people's lives."

When homeowners—if such they could still be called!—were finally allowed to return, they had to pass through an official gridlock to get in. All the people in the burn zone had to have a pass with their names on it. They had to show their identification and prove they lived there. Part of this was to prevent people from looting and stripping copper.

When Nicholas and his wife arrived at their property, it wasn't even recognizable. It was like a snow scene of a war-torn land, the twisted wreckage and vehicle skeletons all covered with white ash.

Nicholas and his wife were expecting their homecoming to be emotional. They were expecting to sob in each other's arms. Instead, they felt a strange numbness. They had already wept when they heard the news, and their tears now seemed to be gone.

The tears did reappear from time to time. The hardest part of the process for Nicholas was burying his dog Ranger. Nicholas had gotten him when he was one month old. At the time of the fire, he was still a puppy, only nine months old. In those eight months, Nicholas had become attached to Ranger and had enjoyed building the personalized log cabin for him. Nicholas did not even like to think about the fire approaching the little dog house. He wept as he dug a hole and buried his puppy.

With the help of volunteers, they began to clean up and sift. Nicholas realized that they had to move on. The ash would not rebuild itself. They would find what they could and then leave.[4]

In the ash they found the family of German glass Hummel people where the reed organ had been. The reed organ on which they were displayed burned to a heap of ash, and the Hummels were found in the heap.

Other artifacts were not so hardy. The sixty-two pieces of cast iron were destroyed. The glass in the windows dripped like icicles.

Nicholas expected to find at least some salvageable books, especially from tightly-piled stacks. He found less than he expected. Walking into the area that had been his library, which was now a three-foot layer of powdery ash, he saw that some of the books were still intact with print visible. Most of them, however, were pure white, and when touched, they turned to powder.

Some of Nicholas's old hymnals from the 1800s survived. They were singed on the outside, but clearly legible. A few *National Geographic* magazines, stacked tight, were not completely destroyed.

With the help of volunteers, they began to clean up and sift. One day in September, with a mask around his neck, an LCRA cap on his head, and the barren wasteland behind him, Nicholas talked about his experience.

"I guess the lesson learned is, *it's all stuff,*" he said. "Your wife and your life with Christ are more important than all your stuff."

Nicholas mentally added "and fire" to Matthew 6:19, the verse that warns against laying up treasure on earth where moth and rust corrupt. "Moth and rust are slow. Fire? That's just fast. You're done," Nicholas said.

In the aftermath of the fire, Nicholas realized that it helped to laugh. "You know that long honey-do list?" he said. "Mine just got shortened. Pow!" Humor was good medicine. He and his friends and family found themselves joking about the fire and the smoke almost every day. It wasn't that the situation was funny. It was just that it was better to laugh than to cry.

Taking charity was neither fun nor funny for Nicholas and his wife. They were not used to it, wanting instead to be the givers. When offered free items, Nicholas's wife hesitated. "We can't take all this soap," she would say. "There are other people who lost their homes."

"You're one of them!" Nicholas would remind her. Sometimes it was necessary to be the one receiving.[5]

It was good that Efrain and Debi did not know on that first night at Debi's sister's house that a new, smaller fire would start the next day. They were able to rest that night.

But on Monday, with confusion at a climax, they heard about the new fire, this time on the west side of Bastrop near the house to which they had escaped. They had to evacuate again.

The same day, the neighbor family who first warned Efrain and Debi lost their own house. Efrain called them to see what was going on. The woman had retreated safely—but her husband? "I'm in a motel room," the woman said. "But that crazy . . . you know how he is," she said apologetically.

"Yes, I know how he is." Efrain couldn't help smiling at the thought of his friend, refusing to evacuate until the last minute.

Efrain and Debi had not yet heard whether their house had burned or not. They kept hoping it hadn't. "Part of you still thinks there's a chance until you see it's gone," they said.

Efrain stayed away from the action for the most part, but Debi wanted to know what was happening. She looked for the list of lost houses and attended the press conferences.

"I was so glad Judge McDonald did the press conferences," she said. The judge was determined to keep people informed. Many people were desperate to get back in and angry that they were being blocked from their own properties. The judge tried to be understanding, but he also explained to them what happens with the trees, about the roots that could burn for days, reaching up to 500 degrees in the stump holes. White ash piles could look cold but be extremely hot. The air itself was filled with toxic emissions.

"It's just too dangerous," Debi heard the judge say. "We lost two people; we're not going to lose another."

Efrain and Debi's house did not show up on the list, so for a long time they didn't know what to expect. Finally, with Debi's sister along, they were able to return to their house site. "Is this our street?" they asked each other.

Their two-story log home could not be seen. They walked around in disbelief, snapping pictures of a place they had never seen before—a place that had once been home.

"Why didn't you take colored pictures?" friends asked them later when they showed them the photos.

"These *are* colored pictures," they said. There was no color left in that part of the world, only black and white.

There was just one item of color left, and Efrain and Debi stared at it in disbelief. It was the vehicle she had parked on the road. There was no melted paint, no scratches, no blistered paint, and no blown tires. She had already gotten the papers from the insurance company for the vehicle, and there it was, as if nothing had happened.

Debi noticed the needles left on the pine trees. They seemed to be melted into a permanent wind-swept shape, as if molded by the intense heat and wind.

Close to a friend's house, they found five charred deer grouped together, apparently caught by the fire as they tried to escape it by hiding. Life wasn't good for the animals that survived either. Efrain and Debi saw a doe and fawn walking through the ash. There was nothing to eat.

Ravines and hollows they never knew existed appeared. They had been cloaked for years in trees and undergrowth. Their home area was now a different place. The Texan tradition of giving directions by landmarks no longer worked. The "A-frame house at the corner" or the "pink house" no longer existed.

> ## HOW BAD WAS IT? MEASURING A FOREST FIRE
>
> It is possible to tell the severity of a forest fire by looking at what is left when the fire is gone. In the Bastrop Complex Fire, various levels of severity were evident.
>
> In lightly burned and scorched areas, most shrubs and trees had survived. The forest floor was still littered with charred needles, small trees, and half-burned logs.
>
> In the moderately burned area, all shrubs were gone and most trees were blackened.
>
> In the most heavily burned areas, the color was a winter-like whiteness. In these worst areas, all organic matter was gone, with only tree trunks remaining. The standing trees had no green left, evidence of a raging crown fire. Even tree trunks that had been lying on the forest floor before the fire were gone, having slowly smoldered from the bottom up, the ash falling off from beneath. The top inch of soil had been incinerated. All trees and shrubs were completely gone, although perhaps some living roots remained that could still produce life. The heavily burned area covered 11,527 acres, or 35 percent of the fire zone.

Alan Donaldson didn't get to his house until the Wednesday or Thursday after the fire. All of his phone chargers were burned, so he didn't have any communication with anyone.

As Alan climbed through the remains of his house, he found it strangely fascinating. If his had been the only house burned, he might have been more upset. He knew he could choose to be angry anyway. But looking at the broad scale on which the fire hit and the hundreds who lost their homes, he felt more a kind of awe than anger.

"Wow, we got creamed," he said matter-of-factly.

He actually found his Egyptian scarab beetle, although its blue coat was burned off. When he first looked at his shelves of books, he thought some had survived. But when he touched them, they crumbled.

René and Kathy Rizk's house went up in flames, but their son's car did not. René was glad that his son had something normal left after losing his newly-remodeled space.

For the Rizks, the worst loss was the memorabilia of their boys as children. It also hurt to have their little granddaughter come looking for things that she remembered having at Grandpas' house.

"We believe God has always been with us," René said. He felt the fire was an attack of Satan, yet God used it for good. The destruction had brought the best out of people, and they could count so many blessings.

Bill and Patsy Ludwig were given a map of the area in which all the destroyed properties were outlined in red. Theirs was not outlined in red, so they knew it was still standing. However, as they went through the house, they realized that it had been permanently stamped with smoke. Everything in the house would have to be taken out and cleaned.

The fire had ravaged the 370 trees. Some of them were able to stay, but dozens had to be cut down and turned into lumber. Patsy and Bill wanted to use the lumber themselves, as much as possible. It would seem right to bring some redemption to the damaged trees.

Patsy dismantled and cleaned her smoky house, but she could still smell smoke for weeks. She grieved the lost shed full of antiques. Patsy missed her neighbors, her trees, and the wild animals. She couldn't sleep well and struggled with fear. When she heard the noise of motors, she remembered the helicopters thumping overhead.

Still, she and her family wanted to stay on their property, and she was not angry at God like many people she knew. She felt that God saved her house for a purpose, placing His protecting hand on the property.

The flames had melted the skirting of the house, yet the house had not ignited.

"God will let me know what that purpose is, what He wants me to do," Patsy told others.

People asked her sometimes how she could be positive, why she wasn't angry at God. She told them she did not feel God caused the disaster, but He walks with His people through tough times.

After the fire, Patsy's old confusion came back on the topic of giving. How was it possible to tell whether someone was lazy or truly poor? She felt that in the post-fire period, government programs rewarded laziness. When she and Bill applied for assistance from FEMA, they received a letter stating that FEMA could not help them because they had really good credit and a nice salary. The Small Business Administration agreed to let them borrow money for 5 percent interest, but if they wouldn't have had a good income, they could have borrowed for 2 percent. Patsy felt that they were penalized for thinking ahead, getting insurance, and saving money.

"The Lord gives us things, but it's our responsibility to take care of them," she mused. "Why do I have to pay taxes to cover for people who failed to get insurance?"

Despite feeling confused, Patsy felt this was one of the only questions that hadn't been answered for her. God had taught her so much through the disaster, and He had stopped the fire even as it melted the skirting of their house.

She felt immensely blessed.

16

HOMES ALONG HIGHWAY 71

When Larry was able to make it back to his property, he discovered that a number of his goats had been killed. The ones who were alive had run up onto the porch of his house. Some of them had burned ears. Others were plagued with respiratory problems, and these goats died one by one from the smoke that had destroyed their lungs.

While Larry was at his property, he discovered a fawn, injured and traumatized by the fire. It was bleeding and burned, and it was so traumatized it was not afraid of Larry. It allowed him to put a handful of his expensive goat feed into its mouth. Next he offered it a bottle of Gatorade, which it guzzled down. Because Larry needed to leave the property, he put the fawn into a small pen with food and water. When he left, the fawn wanted to follow him. But despite his care, the fawn later died from its injuries.

Jimmy Mack had a friend who offered them a camper to stay in.

Jimmy and his wife parked the camper in a campground outside Bastrop and moved in. For the time, it would be home.

Jimmy felt sad when he thought of their possessions going up in smoke. He especially regretted the loss of their passports, filled with stamps from around the world. But he realized they were just things. Besides, the loss had come at a good time in their lives. They were both ready to retire. Jimmy would quit his job on the Geek Squad after Black Friday. His wife would work until March of 2012. Then, instead of buying a new house, they would buy an RV and take a trip through the United States. While traveling, they could decide where to build their next house.

Jimmy and his wife had already been blessed since the fire, even though they were living in a borrowed camper. Before the fire, Jimmy's wife would often talk to him about all the stuff he was accumulating. That was no longer a problem, because the stuff was gone. Besides, they had come up with a new strategy. They would both agree before making any new purchase.

They had no television in their temporary home. Sitting there in the campground without the normal prattle of the television, they had more time to communicate. They learned to talk more. The quiet after the storm had done good things for their marriage.

George and his wife had been planning to take a vacation that September. As they were caught in limbo, not knowing if their house was standing, they discussed their vacation plans.

"Honey, are we going to take a vacation if our house is gone?" George asked his wife.

They concluded they had no reason to stay. They had each other, their two sons, their computers, photos, and dogs. They could let the other material possessions go.

As time went on and homeowners were still not allowed back in,

George was able to go back to his house because he was a firefighter. He was immensely relieved to find his house still standing. As a firefighter, he could also assist friends and strangers. When George was at the convention center looking at the posted maps, people would come up to him and ask, "Is my house there? I have animals!" Friends would give him their keys, and he would go to their houses. He rescued frantic pets in empty houses. The electricity was off, so all the food in refrigerators and freezers was spoiling. To save the appliances, he pitched the spoiling food.

A day before leaving on vacation, George and his wife were able to get back into their house. They packed what they needed and left. George found the vacation well-timed and refreshing. He had not been able to spend time with his boys during the fire, so the vacation was a great time to take a break.

Ryan's minivan was never quite the same after entering the fire zone on a motorcycle path. Betsy still ran, but Ryan knew that one day she would fall apart. He was fascinated to find out that a picture of him evacuating with Betsy appeared on the Internet.

Ryan's house and possessions did not burn, although he lost about a hundred dollars' worth of groceries. He was glad he had been able to help out in the fire. He had seen the action firsthand and had answered countless phone calls from people on the outside.

However, even being the contact person had its emotional impact. Ryan shed many tears as he told the bad news. But even the bad news gave him a chance to help others. He slipped cash to friends who lost their houses and needed motel rooms. He knew that if the emotional toll was hard on him, it must be much worse for others.

Mr. Walters of the animal shelter dealt with anxiety once he moved back to his home. He was terrified of smelling smoke, even if it was just a neighbor's barbecue. He didn't like to hear the wind blowing. He slept with his windows and drapes open so that he could not be surprised by what was going on outside.

At first he thought he was the only one who felt this way. Then he heard the stories of other people and realized he was among friends. "You think you're alone and that you're the only one with those thoughts," he said. "Then you talk to others, and they are going through the same thing."

In spite of being beset with commercial requests, Shirley and the *Bastrop Advertiser* were able to capture much beauty. The *Advertiser* told of random acts of kindness, such as the citizen of Bastrop who received Walmart gift cards from a citizen of Joplin, Missouri, the city devastated by a tornado only months before the Bastrop fires.[1]

Letters to the editor rang with thanksgiving. "Judge McDonald exhibited true leadership and compassion throughout these trying times and is a credit indeed to Bastrop County," one said.[2]

Another said, "I just want to say thank you from the bottom of my heart to everyone who has helped out the mass number of fire victims in Bastrop County. My family lost our home, transportation, and pets. We are shaken to the core, yet everywhere we turn is a silver lining. We are realizing what a caring community we belong to."[3]

On the back of the September 15 edition of the *Bastrop Advertiser* was a quarter-page ad simply titled. It said, "Thank You: To all of the firefighters, rescuers, organizations, and individuals that came from far and local to save lives, homes, pets, equine, and livestock fighting the wildfire of Bastrop and other Texas communities." The person who paid for the ad did not even sign his own name but simply said, "Grateful Red Rock, Texas, resident."[4]

One newspaper employee was also a volunteer firefighter. He shared his heart in an article. He recalled fighting the fire in his own little corner of the world and then going to refuel. On the refueling drive, he saw the fire extended for miles, both north and south. He was one of the first firefighters to lose his home. Then on Tuesday he went to the newspaper office, where he met fellow employees who had lost their homes but also showed up at work.

"During a disaster of this magnitude," he wrote, "it's almost as surreal to be working at a newspaper as it is to be out fighting the fires." Both jobs were a confusing mix of rumor, truth, conflict, and exhaustion. Both were constantly changing.

He ended with a prayer. After reflecting on the house he built with his own hands and the cedar pole that marked his children's yearly heights, he said, "But so much is left . . . so I offer thanks. Thanks that so many found safety in the face of such a ferocious and fast-moving fire. I pray that we grow in kindness, wisdom, and generosity. Rain and time will restore the earth. Love and work will restore our community."[5]

IS A FOREST FIRE ALL BAD?

Rich Gray of the Texas Forest Service says that fire used to be part of the natural world, and our efforts in modern times to prevent fire have actually made wildfires worse.

For many years firefighters had tried to stamp out all forest fires as quickly as they started. Gradually, however, people began to suspect that some fire was necessary to prevent much worse fires. If the small fires were instantly put out, dangerous amounts of underbrush accumulated in the forests. Then when a fire did start, it became explosive.

In 1943 a man named Harold Weaver led the discussion about the sickness of the forests. He said that some fire was healthy for the forests.[6] For a while no one agreed, but by 2011, everyone understood the value of fire to clear out the underbrush in forests. Besides clearing space, fire creates actual benefits to the ecosystem. Grasses grow well after fires, at least if it rains. Some animals benefit directly from forest fires: bark beetles, woodpeckers, rodents, and grass-eating animals like elk and deer.[7]

Fire is necessary to sustain a pine forest. Without fire, oaks eventually would take over and choke out the pines. For the impressive Lost Pines of Bastrop to continue, fires will have to continue—but preferably small, infrequent fires. Small fires create a mosaic forest with patches of different kinds of vegetation.

Greg Creacy of Texas Parks and Wildlife states that small, mosaic-creating fires are a good thing, but this does not mean that the Bastrop Complex Fire was helpful to the environment. Had the Bastrop pines spanned two million acres and had only thirty thousand acres of it burned, it might have been helpful to the overall health of the forest. Instead, the forest lost half of its acreage of pine trees, from a forest that had been decreasing each year before the fire.

In the Bastrop Complex Fire, there were two huge problems that made the fire worse. One problem was that the weather was so hot that the fires did not significantly decrease at night. The other problem was a dense understory, something that could have been consumed gradually by small fires along the way. With the accumulated undergrowth of decades, the fire simply exploded, tossing burning embers eight thousand feet in the air.

To prevent this problem, firefighters try to conduct carefully controlled prescribed burns from time to time. "Designing a prescribed fire is like balancing on a tightrope," says Taylor Morrison.[8] If the fire is too big, it will burn up the big trees that create the forest. If it is too small, it will not burn the brush and shrubs that create the choking effect in unburned woods.

17

REPLANTING AND REBUILDING

Mike Fisher and Judge McDonald were pleased with the people of Bastrop. The people had been sensible enough to escape from the forest fire. There had been only two casualties.

But as the fall of 2011 began, the leaders realized that much work was still ahead. The countryside was black and stripped of trees and grass. The rivers were full of black dust. Piles of trash and burned trunks rose beside the highways. The guardrails lay beside the roads where they had fallen. Sixteen hundred homes and thirty thousand acres had been burned.

Cleaning, restoring, and rebuilding would take much planning and money. Would the people who had been smart enough to escape be smart enough to recover? Would they clean up the wreckage without getting hurt? Would they know how to plant new trees and grass? Would they build new and safer houses?

Mike Fisher, Judge McDonald, and many others in the county did everything they could to give the people ideas about how to clean, restore, and rebuild.

In January they decided to have a special workshop for anyone who wanted to learn more. They held the workshop at McKinney Roughs Nature Park, where Nicholas Cowey worked. The nature park was still green, having escaped the ravages of the fire. The loblolly pine trees were still swaying cheerfully in the wind.

But Nicholas, who opened the meeting, drew the minds of the attendees back to a fire at McKinney Roughs in 2008. It was just a small fire that time, but the thing that Nicholas wanted to bring to attention was what was happening in the present, three years later. In the very part of McKinney Roughs where the fire had occurred, new springs of water had developed, producing more than four gallons of water per minute. The springs had produced about seven and a half million gallons of water since the fire. In the places where the fire had burned the hottest, grasses that normally grew four feet tall were growing up to seven feet tall. Because of the evidence from the past, there was hope that this ecosystem would be restored to a better condition than it had been before the fire.

Next, Mike Fisher recapped the entire drama of the fire in a few brief, powerful sentences. He stated that four minutes before the first fire call, radio traffic recorded this: "Several thousand-acre fires going all over Central Texas threatening homes. Let's get other dispatchers in."

Then, about four minutes after the fire started, the Bastrop Fire Department radioed to the EOC, asking for more help.

About four minutes after that, the decision was made to start evacuations, knowing the fire could not be put out.

About four hours into the fire, the call was made for state and federal response.

About four days later, the burn scar ceased to grow. People and resources were put in place to assess the damage and begin planning for recovery.

Finally, four weeks later, the fire was 100 percent contained and a recovery plan was presented.

"Response and recovery are two different things," Mike explained to the crowd in the McKinney Roughs dining hall. "There isn't always a clear line between the two, but the time measurements are different.

Response is measured in minutes and hours. Recovery is measured with a calendar: days, months, years.

"Four months later, we are done with the response and we are well into the recovery stage. We are not starting recovery now," Mike reminded them. "That was started four days after the 9-1-1 call came through."

At the workshop various departments shared useful tips for the people. There was advice for safety during cleanup, directions for replanting grass and trees, and advice for rebuilding houses and landscapes.

Was it safe to work outside in the dirt and ash when many chemicals and materials from old houses had burned there? The workshop taught that something good had come out of the intense heat of the fire. Many of the contaminants present in buildings—insulation, paint, roofing materials—that might normally leak into the soil, air, or water, literally vanished because the fire was so hot. The soil had been tested, but nothing bad had been discovered. The contaminants were simply incinerated by the tremendous heat.

However, as Mike noted with his typical serious humor, children should not be allowed to eat the ash. He added safety tips such as wearing gloves and long sleeves, or even a respirator in a really bad area. But for the most part, people were much safer in the wildfire zone than they would have been if their house had been burned by a normal structure fire.

Even the water had been tested for poisonous run-off. Water testers dipped water from Alum Creek into a Ziploc bag on October 9, 2011. The water was jet black, as if someone had blended a piece of charcoal into it. But the tests had revealed only suspended ash and sediment, nothing extremely dangerous.

The workshop leaders suggested that the people should leave some debris on the ground, perhaps a fallen log, to provide homes for the many homeless animals. Squirrels, birds, and raccoons were all looking for homes after the fire.

Would it be necessary to plant new trees and grass? Would some trees and grass grow back on their own? The workshop taught that the intense heat of the fire had been bad for the plants. In moderate and heavily burned areas, plants would not reseed on their own because the seeds, roots, and even parts of the soil had been burned away by the intense heat.

Just to purchase seed for grass and plants on public ground would cost $600,000, stated a representative from the environmental group. But if the barren soil was not reseeded, the land would be a target for erosion.

If a huge rain were to descend on the burned countryside, erosion would quickly eat the land. Erosion could start with small things—the force in even one raindrop is considerable, but normally plants keep all of that force from hitting the soil. With the plants gone, the soil was open to destruction by rains, particularly big rains. The fire had made the soil water-repellant in some areas, which could cause the water to simply slide across the top of the soil. What could start with a few grains of silt washing away could progress to a huge gully cutting through roads and landscapes.

A group of volunteers had donated one ton of seed balls. Citizens were allowed to pick up these seed balls for free to help recreate their private landscapes.

At the workshop people were taught to reseed their empty landscapes with native seed. If this did not happen, the empty land would soon grow thick with weeds. Burned pastures should be allowed to regrow through an entire season following a fire, if possible. If the pasture land had to be used the next season, it should not be used until mid-July. When broad-leaf weeds sprouted, which was to be expected, land owners were urged to resist the temptation to spray them.

Besides reseeding the land, attention also had to be given to new trees. Planting trees, while more difficult than seeding grass, was important if the pine forest was going to return. If nothing was done to replant the Lost Pines of Bastrop, the pine forest area would eventually be choked by yaupon and invasive species. Because of this, it would be necessary to "manage" the cedars, oaks, and yaupon to protect the pines. At the post-fire workshop, Daniel Lewis of the Texas Forest Service explained that "manage" was a nice way of saying "kill." If the beautiful pines were going to come back, the other species would have to be removed and new pines planted.

Attendees took small trees home with them to plant. Daniel Lewis gave tips on planting trees. He said 450,000 loblolly pine seedlings were being prepared for the next tree planting.

> ### HOW TO PLANT A PINE SEEDLING
>
> Seedlings should not be purchased until the ground is prepared and all tools are available. If it is necessary to store seedlings, they need to be kept cool and shaded.
>
> A dibble bar should be used to plant pine seedlings. The dibble bar is thrust into the ground to make a hole. After the seedling is carefully planted in the hole, the dibble bar is thrust into the ground again, right beside the first hole, to pack dirt against the roots. Care must be taken that the seedlings are not planted too shallow or too deep, forcing their roots into a J or L shape.

> ### HOW TO PLANT A PINE TREE
>
> If you want a head start on tree growing, plant a tree rather than a seedling. Dig a bowl-shaped hole two to three times wider than the root ball (but not deeper than the root ball). Place the tree in the hole. Backfill the hole with the dirt removed from the hole, without adding any fertilizer, which could burn the tender roots and slow growth. Settle the back-filled dirt with water. Layer three to four inches of mulch or bark chips on top of the tree site, but don't allow the mulch to touch the trunk of the tree. Water the tree every day for two weeks; every other day for two months; then once a week until the tree is well-established beyond doubt, about a year. Use two gallons of water per inch of trunk diameter. In other words, if the tree is two inches wide, give it four gallons of water. If it's a half inch wide, it only needs

> one gallon of water. To protect the tree from animals, place a wire cage around it.
>
> The most important motto for planting trees is "NEVER GIVE UP." If trees die, replant. Tree planting is a gamble, especially in a drought. Irrigate trees when possible, and plans should be made every year to replant for losses.
>
> Tree planting should be matched to the situation. Trees can be used for screens, to surround a home, or to control erosion. But always choose a tree that will be in its natural habitat where conditions are right for it to thrive.

Was there any point in rebuilding houses on the barren landscape? Some people were discouraged and didn't want to rebuild. "How do they expect us to rebuild in an area that looks like downtown Nagasaki in 1945?" a man asked.

Some people wondered about the chances of another fire. The workshop discussed what made the sixteen hundred houses burn while some houses did not burn. Mike recalled that the factors were small but numerous: pine needles on roofs and in gutters, the amount of vegetation around the house, the cleanliness of the roof, the building materials used to construct the house, and proximity to other burning structures. "But still," he admitted, "there are sixteen hundred different reasons why the sixteen hundred houses burned."

> ## THE HARD FACTS OF LOST HOMES
>
> In Bastrop, 1,660 houses and 36 commercial buildings were destroyed. This does not include buildings that were damaged but not destroyed. Within the area where the fire raged, more than half the homes were destroyed. Tahitian Village lost 264 homes, and Circle D Country Acres lost 386 homes.[1]
>
> Economic statistics from previous Texas fires show that not all houses are rebuilt after a fire. One year after a fire,

not even half of the destroyed houses are restored.

ANONYMOUS SUCCESS STORY

One homeowner was on a trip to Houston when the fire started. He reports that their house was one of the few in their neighborhood to be saved.

"Many things went into our home being saved," the homeowner reports. The house was only a year old, so it was up to date with fire codes. Even with these precautions, there were embers in the attic. Also, they had removed twenty-five trees from the lot when they moved in, as well as the underbrush. In addition, when they arrived at their home after the fire, they found that firefighters had thrown lawn furniture away from the house to keep it from combusting and catching the house on fire.

"It was the actions of these men and women and our precautions that prevented our home from the same fate of so many others," the homeowner says.[2]

MAKING A HOME FIRE-WISE

Roofing materials should be fire-resistant: tile, metal, or asphalt. Attic vents and eaves need to be given particular attention, enclosing or screening them so that sparks will not ignite them. Windows should be made of tempered glass with fire-resistant drapes and shutters. No boards, vegetation, or other flammable materials should be left under decks. Gasoline should be stored away from occupied buildings, and garden hoses should be able to hook up to all four sides of a house. All combustibles—picnic tables, stacked lumber, or boats—should be kept away from a house.

On the afternoon of January 9, 2012, Bastrop County Recovery held a forum in the courthouse to review their recovery plan for the county. Mike Fisher was there early, bustling around the room passing out paper agendas. Judge McDonald also circled in and out of the room as citizens began to fill in the seats of the courtroom.

On the schedule were representatives from debris removal, the environmental committee, the roads and bridges people, the finance group, and members of the long-term recovery committee.

The meeting began with a prayer, thanking God for the rain that had come in December, "turning a dark situation to green."

Mike Fisher opened the meeting. Thankfully, the recovery plan adopted ninety days ago was no longer current, he said. Work had been done, and the to-do list had been shortened. The point of the afternoon meeting was to see how much was left to do. Each committee would get a chance to talk about its progress.

The cleaning committee talked first. On county land, such as that beside roads, the committee had already removed ten thousand trees. Private citizens could also request to have their destroyed trees removed by the county. FEMA used spray paint to mark trees not considered safe, and paperwork had to be completed for each property. This amounted to an estimated fifteen thousand sheets of paper for the tree project alone.

The representative for debris cleanup talked about the many complaints he heard about all the rules, regulations, and paperwork. He carried a two-inch binder of regulations and a one-inch binder of receipts from a single day.

"I'm not throwing FEMA under the bus, though," he said. He reminded the audience that often someone cheats the system, forcing FEMA to make a new rule. In the past, contractors had been paid for every load of debris they dumped in the landfill. Some dump trucks would drive in, get paid for their load, then drive out and drive in again, getting paid twice for the same load. Because of this, FEMA had to tighten their regulations. Now there were field monitors, and tickets were cross-checked. A clipboard was lowered from a control tower to each dump truck for the trucks to sign in and out. At the exit of the field, officials ensured that each truck was actually empty.

The representative also reminded everyone that the county did not want to be on bad terms with the government in the end. For five years after receiving disaster grants from the government, Bastrop County would be subject to federal audit. If auditors arrived and saw that the funds were not used appropriately, Bastrop County could be put on the "de-obligated" list of organizations that need to repay the money they were given. He cited a case in which an academy was required to pay back $18,000,000 because of the way they had handled federal money.

"*We* don't want to make that list," he said with certainty.

A representative from the roads and bridges committee spoke next. This committee was most concerned that a big rain would come before the grass and trees had time to regrow. A huge rain could cut through the open soil and split roads in half. "It was like a breath of fresh air when we reseeded along Highway 71," the representative said. He talked about how the guardrails and culverts had melted, but he was grateful that many were replaced already.

The roads received a beating from the heavy equipment that had rattled over them ever since Labor Day. First, the roads were covered with fire engines and bulldozers. In the cleanup phase, endless caravans of dump trucks and county vehicles drove the roads. As rebuilding took place in the future, the roads would take a beating from cement trucks and construction vehicles. Still, the ninety miles of roads were more threatened by erosion than by overuse.

The commissioners then discussed finances and expressed their gratitude for a $5 million gift from the Lower Colorado River Authority. The LCRA had also paid for the printing of a stack of helpful cards for the citizens. These cards had links, tips, and guidelines for homeowners, punched in a corner and joined by a silver ring. There was a card for evaluating pine trees and determining the damage to the crown of the tree. There was a card for tree-planting steps. The cards were color-coded: green for tree cards, brown for erosion and soil fact cards, brown and orange for wildlife cards, and olive green for agriculture fact cards. There was a dark green card for financial assistance and blue cards for general safety, recovery, and health.

Even with the generous gifts and services from the LCRA, the county knew they would run out of funds as they were faced with their daunting tasks. They discussed the grants from FEMA. The federal government usually paid seventy-five cents of every grant dollar. It was common for states to pick up the remaining twenty-five cents. Would the state of Texas help them? They did not know yet.

They had to keep meticulous track of everything for three years: the millions of dollars, thousands of volunteer hours, and hundreds of workers.

Next, a committee talked about volunteers. Nearly fifty thousand volunteer hours had been logged. Church groups came. The Society of St. Vincent de Paul came. House-in-a-box programs helped out. Christian Aid Ministries, described at the meeting as an "awesome group of Mennonites," provided free labor for building houses.

This led to a discussion about home building. Of the 1,660 households who lost homes, 37 percent of them were uninsured. Not all would attempt to rebuild. But would the volunteers be enough to assist the ones who did want to rebuild? And were volunteers sufficient for skilled construction jobs? The houses need to be built well to make them fire-safe in the future.

At the end of the meeting, Judge McDonald thanked everyone for asking how they could help rather than focusing on their own concerns. He reminded the people that other towns were watching Bastrop's response. Would Bastrop be able to survive? "Everyone in the room has to make that commitment to work together moving forward," a commissioner said. He felt confident that the Bastropians would have the attitudes necessary to do so.

FIRE ECONOMICS

Thirty-six commercial structures were destroyed by the fire, and others were damaged.[3] However, even businesses that were not destroyed were affected by the fire. Businesses are affected directly when the fire destroys their machines or buildings or inventory. They are affected indirectly when their customers leave the area, suddenly quit spending money, or suddenly begin spending more money.

After most disasters, construction and demolition companies do really well. However, this is not considered an economic gain in the same way that growth from an increasing population would be, because the gain is merely a response to a larger loss.[4]

In Bastrop, the Sac n' Pac gas station on the corners of Texas Highways 21 and 95 was a flurry of activity after the fires as fire crews from around the country dropped in for necessities and food. Maxine's downtown became a meeting place in the days after the fire. People talked and ate. The same thing happened at the Coffee Dog across from the EOC. The owner offered the Coffee Dog as a place where people could meet and use free Internet, and in return many of them purchased something to eat or drink. Area motels were afloat with evacuated or homeless Bastropians.

Businesses that didn't involve food or shelter or home repair were a different story. Business that marketed entertainment or discretionary products suffered immediately after the fire. The golf course in Bastrop State Park was closed for two weeks and then only opened part-time. Even then, rumors were circulating that it had been destroyed. The golf course operated at a loss.

Dixie's Den of Antiques near Alum Creek Drive was a business in the heart of the burn area. The business reopened after being closed for three weeks, but sales diminished. The owner reported that customers now buy fewer and smaller items, perhaps because they are living in small, temporary homes or FEMA trailers. However, the sales continue to trend upward. Considering the number of antiques lost in the fire, it's not hard to imagine that once owners are in their new houses, they will want to buy antiques to replace the ones they lost.[5]

Bluebonnet Electric Cooperative, one of the state's largest electric providers, also took a hit. Even before the fire was contained, they began efforts to repair and replace 4,300 electric meters. They also replaced 1,223 burned poles and 61 miles of electric wire at a price of $7,105,268.[6]

Compared to historic fires in California, the total dollars lost in Bastrop are smaller, but the loss per person in Bastrop County is greater, because it is a small county. Fires in Oakland and San Diego caused millions of dollars of damage but were divided across counties with populations of one or two million.

In 2010, there were 74,171 people in Bastrop County. The total loss from the fire is estimated at $209,318,741. This averages out to a cost of $2,822 per person, higher than the large California fires. This makes the Bastrop Complex Fire the largest per capita wildfire loss in the nation's history at the time of the 2011 report.[7]

18

CHRISTMAS AND NEW HOUSES

Christmas 2011 was approaching. Debra's friend Holly was finally getting a new house delivered after a four-month wait. As happy as Debra was for her friend, the ache of being left behind was great. She and Holly had gone through this whole process together, and now Holly had moved on.

In the meantime Debra was getting to know the neighbors around her temporary home. Next door, she met a young lady wearing a five-pointed pentagram, a Wiccan symbol shaped like a star. Instantly Debra remembered her days in the occult shop among the incense and tarot cards.

Although Debra hated what she considered the "lost time" spent in the occult shop, she had found that people were often willing to listen to her story. At the One Day Academy where she taught, Debra would sometimes hear students mention the horoscope.

"You think it's okay for you to read your horoscope every day," she said. "But all that does is get you comfortable with divination. I'll tell you why the Lord abhors divination. You start going to your horoscope to find out what to do with your life instead of coming to the Lord.

Satan is very evil but very patient."

As a teenager, Debra began to read the newspaper horoscope. *Oh, I'm a Pisces,* she realized. She followed the horoscope with interest, and she also found out there were books about being a Pisces.

"Satan doesn't care what you run to as long as it's not God," Debra told her students one day, reflecting on her own experiences. She stated that the biggest hindrance for most people is giving up their own personal agenda. It requires a new thought process, a new personal identity, to follow God. Debra had struggled with knowing who she would be if she turned to God. She remembers thinking, *If I turn my back on being a witch and tell everyone I was living a lie, who am I [now]?* She had worshipped John Lennon; consequently, getting rid of her music was the hardest thing.

Now she hoped to influence the neighbor girl with the Wiccan star and help her to know truth. The girl liked Debra but was disappointed when she found out Debra was a Christian.

"It's such a shame, because I really liked her," the girl told her mother. "Every other Christian I've met tells me that I'm going to hell."

Debra, on the other hand, remembered her own journey and felt sure that Jesus Christ would reach this girl at the right time. She noticed that the girl and her family were struggling. It was almost Christmas, and they had no money. Their house was infested with German cockroaches, like hers had been. Then the girl hit a deer and totaled her car.

"I think the Lord wants us to help them," Dean said. "There are just too many parallels." People had been generous to Dean and Debra following the loss of their house. They wanted to pass on the blessings, and they did have money in their checking account.

Dean and Debra started by ordering a series of bug treatments and buying a carload of groceries and Christmas items. The surprise and gratitude on the faces of the neighbors was overwhelming.

"It's so funny to think that two hundred dollars could solve someone's problem," Debra mused. But she remembered the Christmas several years earlier when fifty dollars had enabled her to buy gifts for her family.

It had been the leanest Christmas of all. The family was broke. Debra had a college degree, and people told her that she should work. But Debra felt called to stay at home and homeschool their children, and Dean supported her in that decision.

One day Debra helped decorate the church for a Christmas event with the other church ladies. Everyone was chatting about the gifts they would buy for their children and the decorating they would do. Finally Debra had to step outside for a bit to hide her deep grief and embarrassment.

A caring older lady had walked out to see what was wrong, and Debra confided what was bothering her. The next Sunday at church, the lady personally handed her an envelope with fifty dollars slipped inside. With joy, Debra had pulled out her calculator to see just how thinly she could spread the gift.

Recalling their blessings, Dean and Debra wanted to do more for their neighbor family. "We need to find a way to get something for them to drive," Dean said. He called Howard, whom they teased about having the "spiritual gift of Internet." Dean told him that they needed to find an inexpensive but dependable car. By that night Howard had located a car—and it was close by.

While the men picked up the car, Debra slipped over to the neighbors to tell them that there was something coming. When the car pulled in, the neighbors said, "Is it something we need to help carry in? Is it in the trunk?"

"No, here it is," said Dean, putting the keys in the young woman's hand.

"You're kidding."

"No—I'm serious."

Through tears, the neighbors asked why they had done this.

"Because God is good. He loves you."

There were no strings attached from Debra's end. The girl did not become a Christian. But Debra was just glad that, at this post-fire Christmas holiday, she was able to show what the love of Christ really looked like. The Lord had allowed Debra to bless someone as she herself had been blessed.

Debra's daughter Jorja spent some time with the younger daughter from the same house. Once the little girl asked, "What's a Bible?" And Jorja brought them three little Bibles, two blue ones and a brown one.

Debra's sons also asked if they could invite the neighbors to church one Sunday morning, which they did. "I kind of wanted to come, but it was nice to be asked," the grandma said, and she and the little girl went with them.

So the Christmas holidays were more real to Debra than they had ever been before the fire. Christmas itself was spent with Holly's family in their new house. "I was more aware of Christmas—every little piece of Christmas," Debra said of the 2011 holidays.

The Christmas party, in a way, was the same as it had always been before, yet Debra noticed that everyone had changed. "We were all different people than we were the year before," she said. "Our fellowship was richer and deeper. We would laugh, and we would listen. It was warm and beautiful—bittersweet in a way, but really, really sweet."

In January the concrete was poured for Dean and Debra's new house. Christian Aid Ministries agreed to build the house with volunteer work crews. They chose to rebuild on the same spot, right there under the blackened pines beside the little oak tree that held the pickle swing that did not burn.

January 13 was a day of victory for Debra and her family. The morning sun had risen on a bare cement slab. The afternoon sun, shining through damaged pine limbs, was setting on a building with four walls, towering beside chopped stumps sprayed with green spray paint.

Their uncle stopped by to investigate. "This is going to be the living room . . . the kitchen . . . the bathrooms," Debra explained with anticipation, walking through the framed rooms.

"We'll be able to have Bible studies now," Dean added.

They were definitely going to put the pickle swing up again too.

Mike Gibbons had no doubt that more people could have saved their properties like he did. However, it was a personal decision on his part, impacted by his experience in emergency services, his wealth of historical items, and the availability of huge water supplies.

Shirley was not so confident that what they had done was wise. She didn't doubt her husband's experience. But there was a big difference between having experience and having the right tools available to put that experience to use. Tennis shoes and garden hoses were not the right tools, and both had melted while in use. But they had survived, and that was the important thing.

On New Year's Eve, Margaret begged God for direction as she walked around the property. They were trying to decide where to place their new house. Finally God gave them peace about the location to rebuild.

Over the Christmas holidays Bastrop received rain. Margaret and Wesley had planted rye grass, a strong ground cover that holds back erosion and doesn't freeze. This beautiful yellow-green grass sprouted out of the jet black, carpeting the ruin with color. Even the leaves remaining on the trees, which often did not change much color in the fall, turned beautiful colors that year.

As a backhoe pushed over the blackened trees, Margaret scraped aside the sand and picked out pieces of rice china and a shard of pottery. She knew that her china hutch must have been right there.

The process of building took longer than the Peschkes expected. But through it all, Wesley and Margaret gave thanks for God's peace and strength.

In January CAM's volunteers arrived. With their base on the southwest side of Bastrop in a campground, they fanned out into the community with tool trailers. They went to the site of Patty Timmons' old home and got to work.

They poured the cement pad and framed the walls. Patty's elation spilled over amid the music of saws and hammers ushering her into the New Year. The bright new wood rose behind the charred stumps and the blackened cast iron patio set she had saved from the rubble. She laughed and cried with joy, giving tours of the partially framed house to anyone who was interested. She would point out the wide window she hoped to frame in white curtains, and the spacious bedroom.

Someone told Patty she was inspirational. "No, I'm not inspirational," Patty laughed. "I'm just stubborn. I was determined; I had two acres of land here."

She gave thanks to God. She praised Paige Webb, the volunteer coordinator who told her she would go to Plan Z if she had to. She was grateful for Christian Aid Ministries and the young men from around the nation who built her house with free labor while she watched.

She knew she could not have done it on her own, and her gratitude spilled over constantly.

By the end of October, Adam and Cindy had a trailer placed on their property. Moving back to their property was hard, though. It could hardly be called moving back, since it was more like moving to an unfamiliar desert.

On Thanksgiving Day, the family attended a church dinner. Their son from Bastrop brought them a turkey. Their other son and his family had moved to Germany. Cindy's family was distant, as usual.

Cindy was disappointed by the response of her family. When the fires hit, they had responded with minimal care. Their coolness toward her widened the rift that had formed when Cindy became a Christian. They did offer some help, but not the moral support Cindy really craved. Other people acted more like family to Cindy than her own. But in this crisis she remembered something she had learned from her grandmother.

"Grandma always talked about the enemy to me in Spanish. She'd say, 'If you don't forgive, God's not going to forgive you!' "

Then, a few days before Christmas, Cindy became ill. She went to her doctor.

"Mrs. Cruz," the doctor said, "you are very sick." In healthy people, oxygen percentage levels are in the upper 90s. The levels in people with chronic lung diseases drop into the 80s. Cindy's oxygen levels dropped into the 70s.

The doctor sent Cindy to the hospital. There she was put on oxygen twenty-four hours a day. Cindy, who had rarely had a fever in her life, spiked a temperature of 102. Cindy lost her voice to the point where Adam was the only person who could understand what she was saying. Doctors suspected she had a stroke.

On a Wednesday night, Cindy's church prayed for her. After that, she was able to take the oxygen off. Cindy suspected the doctor thought she was just being stubborn and did not want to wear the oxygen anymore, but he was amazed when she really didn't need it. "Someone up there is looking out for you," he said.

On Christmas Eve, Cindy came home. "I teared up over Christmas," she freely admits. "I would break down and then realize that the devil was trying to get me discouraged. God blessed us a lot . . . with people in our lives before the fires and after the fires. Waking up every day is a blessing!

"Has it been easy? No. Whether good or bad, we don't stop praising God. I know my faith is more important than anything."

The holidays were approaching, and the Coweys attended a family reunion. They came home with $1,600. A family from church left for a six-week vacation and offered the Coweys their house while they decided what to do next.

Then, Nicholas's years as a Boy Scout leader and a tour guide for McKinney Roughs began to pay off. A Boy Scout friend collected nearly $14,000 of cash and gift cards for the Coweys. A school group in Houston that had come to McKinney Roughs on field trips was doing a unit on empathy. They also took up a collection and sent a money tree worth $4,000.

Nicholas says that he purchased their new house with eleven minutes to spare. Before he went to look at the house, he told the owner to draw up a contract for him just in case he wanted it.

Then he drove to the house and met with the owner. As he began to walk through the house, he asked, "Where's that contract? My wife needs a place to live."

He was signing the contract when the owner's phone rang. The caller announced that he was coming in eleven minutes and wanted to buy the house.

Nicholas also credits some of the strength they had to face the fire to their recent study of the book of Job. Looking at intense suffering and loss before their own suffering had been a gift of God.

Using partially burned pages from hymn books, Nicholas created a fire memorial. He doesn't want to forget this difficult time of their lives.

Most exciting of all, on July 2, 2012, Nicholas and his wife became parents of a son whom they named James Edward. God had blessed them beyond measure.

Alan Donaldson chose to rebuild on his same property. Although the property was the same, a bizarre menagerie of plants sprouted on his lot: corn, poppies, a few sycamore trees, twenty oak trees, and buffalo grass. He had planted none of them, and he could think of no explanation for their presence.

"I tend to adapt to my environment instead of having my environment adapt to me," he said. But nearly a year after the fire, he admitted that his yard looked less like a recovering yard and more like a budding rain forest.

The builder of Alan's new house took Alan to see houses he had built that had survived the fire. "Kind of a compelling selling point," Alan admitted.

He chose a unique design with exposed beams and a vaulted ceiling, something like a fifteenth-century monastery, and big enough to house lots of books. He broke away from the theme for the kitchen, though, using stainless steel and tile for a more modern look.

Kathy Rizk had a birthday in October. For the occasion, her friends banded together to make framed art to replace the pieces she lost from her walls. Using pictures from other sources, the friends created new framed family portraits. They also helped to replace the Christmas decorations Kathy lost in the fire, so that the coming holidays would not be gloomy.

After the fire, Bill and Patsy Ludwig were blessed by an abundance of birds. They put out birdseed, and it got eaten by the bags full as the birds scavenged for food in the empty forest. They estimated that they had four times as many birds as they had before. Even though feeding them took some financial commitment, Bill and Patsy counted the birds a great blessing. The squirrels also came in droves for the sunflower seeds she put out. Patsy believed that God had given her a purpose in life as a caretaker, for people as well as animals.

Patsy was concerned about her neighbor, who was building a giant commercial-sized steel structure. In the steel building, he planned to build his house and park all his vehicles and possessions. It looked as though he couldn't trust in God's goodness and felt the need to protect his possessions at all costs. Patsy wondered where he would put flowers or a garden. She imagined him coming home day after day to a steel building that shut out the world.

Since she couldn't sleep well and got up early, Patsy spent time reading her Bible. Her family had a history of depression, and she took medication for it herself. Yet she found that it worked better to combine physical medicine with spiritual sustenance. Pointing to her Bible, she testified, "This works better than medicine. Everything is here, and it's up to me to search and interpret it. God did not promise ease. Sometimes it takes turmoil to make us realize how fortunate we really are."

Patsy enjoyed taking visitors to the side of her lawn to show them something special. There on the forest floor were pine seedlings she had found, less than a foot tall, reaching toward heaven. Patsy marked each of them with a pink flag and watered them dutifully. Her family was skeptical that the trees would survive, but Patsy kept on watering. For her, the green sprigs were a sign of hope on an empty forest floor.

All around their property, signs of recycling abounded. A cedar bench was handcrafted from one of the large trees destroyed in the fire, and piles of bright new lumber from the same trees resided expectantly around the yard. Patsy and her family wanted to use as many of their own resources as they could.

Larry had problems with his insurance company. The insurance adjuster insisted that since he had a fence between his house and his nine barns, the barns could not be counted as outbuildings. For a while, Larry thought that he was being treated unfairly by the adjuster, but when he inquired in the neighborhood, he found that many others had been told the same thing.

Larry's daughter recovered his melted riverboat. The aluminum shape was so striking that she placed it above her fireplace as artwork.

Of the goats that had gotten sick due to the fire, the last one died at the beginning of January. Larry's herd of goats had lost many members, but he still had some survivors with which to start over.

It had been hard for Jimmy to go on vacation from Bastrop in the past, with the pine trees whispering in the breeze. Bastrop itself had been one of the most beautiful places in the world, but it had become a wasteland overnight. Jimmy and his wife were leaving for a tour of the United States. That would give them time to decide whether or not they should return and rebuild in Bastrop.

The memories were horrific. Jimmy stated that the fire was the worst thing that had happened to him in his life. The way houses and trees blew up would be forever embedded in his mind. Yet Jimmy determined they would not live in the past, pining away for what had once been.

They watched some of their friends live in the past, unable to move on from the loss of their homes and possessions. Jimmy didn't think it was healthy. He planned to jump into the future and face the next adventure with enthusiasm, even if it would be a free fall for a while.

George Martinez stated that the one big lesson he learned from the fire was the need to know insurance companies. The Bastrop Complex Fire showed which insurance companies were fair and which were greedy. In a normal house fire, temperatures remain low enough to preserve the foundation of the building. In the case of the Bastrop Complex Fire, temperatures were so high that foundational damage likely occurred in at least some instances. Most insurance companies were not accustomed to paying out additional money for a new foundation, and some were more willing than others to provide that benefit.

George continued to work for the Bastrop Fire Department and to hang his fire coat on its red rack at Station #2. This station sported new wall décor since the fire. A framed poster of the Bastrop Complex Fire scar graced the wall, with large letters labeling the different divisions of the fire. Fiery photos were inserted under the plastic protector.

 Also adorning the wall were two huge paintings created from a palette of black, white, gray, orange, and yellow. They showed firefighters directing their hoses into an orange and black blaze. All over the canvases, signatures and notes of gratitude were written in white or black pens. *Thank you and God bless all the firefighters. You have done so much and we are so grateful. Thank you for your care and sacrifice. We appreciate you!*

19

THE TOWN THAT HAS ALWAYS SURVIVED

On a cold night in January 2012, about half a year after the Complex Fire, the Bastrop firefighters are going about their normal routines when a fire call blares over their pagers. Darkness has settled over Bastrop County—over its black and leafless forests, lonely chimneys, and brand new houses.

Station #1 responds first, being the closest. Inside, the station's guestbook wall entries have multiplied, nearly covering the entire wall. The guest entries now surround the thermostat and the light switches and almost bump against the green trim of the doorway. There isn't really any room for another big fire on the guestbook.

Their fire truck lumbers past the cast iron firefighter statue on its way to the scene.

Up at Station #3, Alan Donaldson leaps into Engine One, and two other firefighters join him. Everyone buckles in. Four radios are fastened in a row inside the truck, ready for action. The sirens blare and the lights whirl.

The huge vehicle lumbers onto Texas FM 1441, rounding corners with the roar of engine brakes. Above Alan's head, rows of green lights blink into the darkness. The radio crackles with updates.

A fire alarm is sounding at the Home Depot in Bastrop. This is routine, but someone on scene thinks they can smell smoke. This intensifies the situation. Home Depot on fire? Never a good thing!

The firefighter in the back says, "Hey, we took on the Complex Fire." Home Depot is a big store, but perspective is needed—it's nowhere near the size of the Complex Fire.

The radio conversation crackles on. Station #1 firefighters are already on scene, checking things out. They don't smell smoke, and Engine One is instructed to continue non-emergency. Alan cuts the lights and sirens. Over the radio words like *drain, pressure,* and *pump* are heard. Apparently, something is wrong with the sprinkler system at Home Depot.

The bulky engine lumbers down the divided highway and cuts down Highway 95 to Highway 71. In the darkness, the bright lights of CVS Pharmacy and HEB grocery store stand out. The fire engine takes an exit and drives into the Home Depot parking lot. Home Depot employees cluster uncertainly. Customers have been asked to leave.

Home Depot has been a place of safety and recovery for many Bastrop citizens. It's been a place to get life back together, to fix damage, or start from scratch after the huge fire. Now, it's unsettling to be asked to leave this place because of a fire alarm.

The fire alarm continues to ring. Inside the large store, bright alarm lights are flashing on the ceiling. Firefighters in orange coats walk between piles of lumber. They gather at the back of the building in the sprinkler system room, where the pumps and valves are controlled. The firefighters cluster here amid huge black and red pipes covered with dust and cobwebs.

Through an outside door is the back parking lot, where several fire trucks have parked. If there would be a fire, they would use their hoses to connect the Home Depot sprinkler system to the hydrant system. But there's no fire, and they just need to figure out what's wrong.

The night is so cold that fingers freeze without protection. The wind is still, and the stars hang over Bastrop like interested friends. What a journey from the fourth of September, when even at night the temperature refused to drop and the winds refused to die down.

With some investigation, they figure it out. Water pressure has dropped in the sprinkler system, causing the alarm. The pressure will need to be built up before the ringing will go off again.

Finally the ringing quits, and the firefighters pack up to head home.

It's a good night to talk shop, to recount previous emergency calls. The firefighters talk about guardrails and cutting trees. There's no wind tonight, no intense heat, no fires glowing orange, and no massive gray cloud.

On the eastern horizon, however, they spot an orange glow. "I thought that was a fire for a second," one of the firefighters laughs.

It's the moon—a beautiful orange moon "the size of Texas." The night glows, but thankfully not with fire. It glows because of the moon, yellow lines, reflective road signs, and the new guardrails beside the Highway 21 corridor as Engine One rushes up the aisle between the blackened forests. But all forests are black at night, and at this moment it doesn't matter that they are black from ash and charcoal. If Alan looks up tonight, he will see the stars close at hand—no massive cloud is hiding them.

There's a roaring noise, but it's not a crown fire rushing through the tops of the loblolly pines. It's just the roar of the engine brakes as the massive piece of machinery navigates the turn at Terry's Corner, the gas station rumored to have blown up in the complex fires.

Like Bastrop, it is still standing.

In July of 2012, the rest of Bastrop is green. In a verdant pasture on the end of Cardinal Drive, black beef calves scamper to the corner of the barbed wire fence. They dance in the shadow of acres of dead pines, still standing with their blackened heads against the sky.

The Colorado River slides past the cement pillars of Bastrop's bridges.

The river is the color of coffee with a little cream. Water bugs skate across its chocolate top, moving against the current, potentially encountering head-on collisions with clumps of grass following the current. Banks along both sides are lined with trees hung thick with green vines in a nearly jungle effect. Joggers plod up and down the sidewalks that cut through green lawns beside the river.

Patty Timmons is comfortably settled in her new house. It has been almost a year since she left her previous house and came back to find it gone. The front gate and gateposts have been repainted, but the gatepost on the left remains a fire souvenir. Almost half of it was eaten away by the fire, leaving a jagged charcoal bite. The paint was simply added around the burn scar, and the gatepost stayed strong.

Stepping stones in the grass lead up to Patty's green house with dark red trim. On the siding Patty posted a sign that says, "The House That Love Built," made for her by a friend. Patty has photographs of Vernon and Mary Ellen of CAM posting the sign on her house and dedicating the house to God.

Inside the house Patty posted another plaque. "By wisdom a house is built, and by understanding it is established; by knowledge the rooms are filled with all precious and pleasant riches" (Proverbs 24:3-4 ESV). The words are written above a painting of houses and trees.

At the end of her hallway, Patty posted a metal Lone Star, stamping Texan authenticity on the little green house. On the floor of her new living room, Patty displays sun catchers she made from fire debris. Green and blue gemstones are skillfully enclosed in artistic frameworks of rusted wire.

Patty loves her cupboard space, and she loves her backyard. When she steps onto the lawn, Shadow, the brown and white dog that escaped the fire with her, darts around her feet, barking and yipping.

On the deck, terra cotta pottery and bags of potting soil witness to a work in progress. Beyond, clusters of black-eyed Susans and other wildflowers spring up around a rusted metal butterfly sculpture and cast iron patio chairs. She's feeding the birds and squirrels with seeds.

"My sunflowers were as big as dinner plates this year," Patty says. "I've never seen anything like it in my life."

By the summer of 2012, the Pahlows have met their goal. They are holding Bible studies in their new house. On a balmy evening, cars pull into Alum Creek Court and down the slight slope into the Pahlows' circle drive. Small children bounce on a trampoline, and geese waddle around the front door, interested in what's going on. The "stormy cross," blackened by fire, is posted prominently in the charred stump of a destroyed tree. It stands like a triumphant beacon that all is well.

Inside, a long wooden table fills the dining area, and people crowd around it with their Bibles open. Coffee, iced tea, popcorn, and tiny blueberry muffins are being served. Light is slanting through the west windows. The air conditioning is on, and the ceiling fans are whirring happily.

The evening starts with prayer requests and praise. After a prayer, everyone turns to 1 Samuel 23-26, and together the group reads all four chapters.

The group is a mixture of old and young, both physically and spiritually. There's an old man with lots of facial hair, as well as a baby toddling around the table. The Pahlow children sit quietly with their friends around the bar in the kitchen, eating popcorn and also reading along.

Some of the people have been Christians for years and are familiar with the story of Saul. "It's like Saul had ADD or Alzheimer's," someone offers.

Others are brand-new believers. "Is this David the one who was in the lion's den?" someone asks.

The gentle correction is made—Daniel, not David—but the person takes it well, face glowing with the joy of the Lord despite the mistake.

On a July evening Stan Miller is cooking homemade jalapeño poppers on his grill in the darkened parking lot of Celebration Church. The 160 poppers are crammed side by side across the two levels of the grill. The jalapeño peppers have been seeded and cleaned, stuffed with cream cheese, and wrapped in bacon. Toothpicks hold them together as they roast over the coals. Volunteers from Indiana, staying at the church, stream into the parking lot like the bands of light leaking through the glass doors.

"You can only have one," they tease each other as the aroma of the poppers fills the air.

Volunteers are not as common anymore, since the fire is a year in the past. However, occasional volunteers still arrive. Directed by Clint Friesen and Stan Miller, the group from Indiana goes out to construction sites and assists with restoration.

On these work sites shovels scrape away the dirt, preparing holes for cement cookies. Lumber clacks, a skill saw screams, and hammers tap out rhythms under the Texas sun. A light breeze dips into the clearing, fanning the workers and the watchers sitting on stacks of bright lumber.

At another site girls in colorful dresses armed with screw guns and a bright yellow level use a spacer to set and fasten spindles onto the railings of a new deck. Sixteen-year-old boys screw down treads. The experienced construction leader snaps chalk lines and flips utility knives with frightening skill.

"Grandma, come and look!" cries a child. "They work really hard!"

"Yes, they do," agrees the grandma.

The two step out on the newly completed wheelchair ramp, fresh with bright yellow boards. When it's time for a break, the random construction crew sits on whatever is available—boards, paint buckets, or just the Texan forest floor littered with bits of broken glass. They eat slabs of round bologna and homemade chocolate chip cookies in Ziploc bags that their mothers sent along.

"Where are y'all from?" the grandma asks.

"Indiana," someone says, dryly adding, "It's a little bit of a drive."

"I just want to thank you all for the wonderful job you are doing. I can't thank you enough."

Before getting back to work, the girls throw water at each other, trying to prolong the delightful break. The sun shines down on them through the loblollies, some blackened and some green.

The inferno in the Lost Pines has become another milestone in Bastrop's history of survival. The firefighters, the state and federal leaders, and the Bastropians have labored to redeem the effects of a disastrous event. As the volunteers add their efforts to the cause, they cannot know what Bastrop was like before September 4, 2011. They can, however, improve the current situation—looking forward, just like the city itself.

ENDNOTES

Chapter One

[1] "Journal of Stephen F. Austin on His First Trip to Texas, 1821," *The Quarterly of the Texas State Historical Association,* Vol. 7, Texas State Historical Association, Austin, Texas, 1904, p. 295, <http://books.google.com/books/reader?id=mNQ1AAAAIAAJ&printsec=frontcover&output=reader&source=gbs_atb_hover&pg=GBS.PA295>, accessed on June 26, 2013.

[2] *In the Shadow of the Lost Pines: A History of Bastrop County and Its People,* Bastrop Historical Society, Bastrop, Texas, 1955, p. 8.

[3] Ibid., p. 11.

[4] "Chestnut Street Medallions" (pamphlet), funded by Bastrop Economic Development Corporation, Bastrop, Texas.

[5] "Bastrop and Buescher State Parks" (brochure), Texas Parks and Wildlife, 2011, <http://www.tpwd.state.tx.us/publications/pwdpubs/media/pwd_br_p4505_043p.pdf>, accessed on June 24, 2013.

[6] Lower Colorado River Authority, "McKinney Roughs Nature Park," 2012, <http://www.lcra.org/parks/developed_parks/mckinney_roughs.html>, accessed on June 24, 2013.

[7] Karen Ridenour et al., *The Bastrop Complex Wildfire: A Case Study,* Texas Forest Service and Bastrop County Office of Emergency Management, May 2012, Foreword.

Chapter Four
[1] Rich Gray et al., *Wilderness Ridge Fire: A Case Study,* Texas Forest Service, March 25, 2009, p. 1.
[2] Taylor Morrison, *Wildfire,* Houghton Mifflin Company, Boston, 2006, p. 6.
[3] NOAA National Climatic Data Center, "Palmer Hydrological Drought Index," <http://www.ncdc.noaa.gov/oa/climate/research/prelim/drought/phdiimage.html>, accessed on March 15, 2012.

Chapter Five
[1] Lower Colorado River Authority, *Bastrop County Complex Fire* (documentary), production of Hahn, Texas, 2011.

Chapter Six
[1] William H. Cottrell, Jr., *The Book of Fire,* 2nd ed., Mountain Press Publishing Company, Missoula, Montana, 2004, p. 3.
[2] Lower Colorado River Authority, *Bastrop County Complex Fire* (documentary), production of Hahn, Texas, 2011.
[3] Mark Gwin, "Of Love and Loss," *The Bastrop Advertiser,* September 15, 2011, p. A5.
[4] Lower Colorado River Authority, *Bastrop County Complex Fire* (documentary), production of Hahn, Texas, 2011.

Chapter Seven
[1] Kenneth Kesselus, *History of Bastrop County, Texas, Before Statehood,* Austin Jenkins Publishing Company, Bastrop, Texas, 1986, p. 171.
[2] Ridenour et al., *The Bastrop Complex Wildfire: A Case Study,* p. 159.

Chapter Eight
[1] *The Bastrop Advertiser,* September 10, 2011, photo on p. B6.

Chapter Nine
[1] Ridenour et al., *The Bastrop Complex Wildfire: A Case Study,* p. 160.
[2] Morrison, *Wildfire,* p. 27.
[3] Ibid.
[4] Cottrell, *The Book of Fire,* 2nd ed., p. 50.

Chapter Ten
[1] Ridenour et al., *The Bastrop Complex Wildfire: A Case Study,* p. 160.

Chapter Eleven
[1] Morrison, *Wildfire*, p. 32.
[2] Ibid., p. 34.
[3] Ridenour et al., *The Bastrop Complex Wildfire: A Case Study*, p. 23.

Chapter Twelve
[1] *The Bastrop Advertiser*, September 15, 2011, p. A7.
[2] *The Bastrop Advertiser*, September 10, 2011, p. A5.

Chapter Fourteen
[1] Ridenour et al., *The Bastrop Complex Wildfire: A Case Study*, p. 93.
[2] Cottrell, *The Book of Fire*, 2nd ed., p. 52.

Chapter Fifteen
[1] *The Bastrop Advertiser*, September 8, 2011, p. B1.
[2] *The Bastrop Advertiser*, September 10, 2011, p. A4.
[3] "About Texas Attorney General Greg Abbott," November 13, 2012, <https://www.oag.state.tx.us/agency/agga_bio.shtml>, accessed on June 24, 2013.
[4] Seth Prescott (creator), "Bastrop-Fire-Relief Assistance," September 30, 2011, <http://www.youtube.com/watch?v=14mMFEgbcYE>, accessed on June 24, 2011.
[5] Ibid.

Chapter Sixteen
[1] *The Bastrop Advertiser*, September 15, 2011, p. A10.
[2] *The Bastrop Advertiser*, September 10, 2011, p. A4.
[3] Ibid.
[4] *The Bastrop Advertiser*, September 15, 2011, p. A18.
[5] Ibid.
[6] Morrison, *Wildfire*, p. 12.
[7] Ibid., p. 7.
[8] Ibid., p. 36.

Chapter Seventeen
[1] Ridenour et al., *The Bastrop Complex Wildfire: A Case Study*, p. 14.
[2] Ibid., p. 163.
[3] Ibid., p. 14.
[4] Ibid., p. 153.
[5] Ibid., p. 154.
[6] Ibid., p. 155.
[7] Ibid., pp. 12–14.

ABOUT THE AUTHOR

Katrina Hoover is a writer and registered nurse from northern Indiana. She grew up in central Wisconsin with two brothers and three sisters, all of whom developed a love for words through the coaching and example of their parents. Katrina's mother published a variety of books and art, including *The Basics and More Cookbook,* before passing away in 2010 from breast cancer.

As of July 2013, Katrina is a night nurse on the heart floor at Elkhart General Hospital. She enjoys interacting with her patients and hearing about their lives. Every week, she meets a patient or two about whom another book could be written.

Katrina is the author of *Blue Christmas* and *Shatterproof,* both published by Christian Aid Ministries. She welcomes responses from her readers and can be contacted at Katrina@500-words.com. You may also write to her in care of Christian Aid Ministries, P.O. Box 360, Berlin, Ohio 44610.

CHRISTIAN AID MINISTRIES

Christian Aid Ministries was founded in 1981 as a nonprofit, tax-exempt 501(c)(3) organization. Its primary purpose is to provide a trustworthy and efficient channel for Amish, Mennonite, and other conservative Anabaptist groups and individuals to minister to physical and spiritual needs around the world. This is in response to the command ". . . do good unto all men, especially unto them who are of the household of faith" (Galatians 6:10).

Each year, CAM supporters provide approximately 15 million pounds of food, clothing, medicines, seeds, Bibles, Bible story books, and other Christian literature for needy people. Most of the aid goes to orphans and Christian families. Supporters' funds also help clean up and rebuild for natural disaster victims, put up Gospel billboards in the U.S., support several church-planting efforts, operate two medical clinics, and provide resources for needy families to make their own living. CAM's main purposes for providing aid are to help and encourage

God's people and bring the Gospel to a lost and dying world.

CAM has staff, warehouse, and distribution networks in Romania, Moldova, Ukraine, Haiti, Nicaragua, Liberia, and Israel. Aside from management, supervisory personnel, and bookkeeping operations, volunteers do most of the work at CAM locations. Each year, volunteers at our warehouses, field bases, DRS projects, and other locations donate over 200,000 hours of work.

CAM's ultimate purpose is to glorify God and help enlarge His kingdom. ". . . whatsoever ye do, do all to the glory of God" (1 Corinthians 10:31).

THE WAY TO GOD AND PEACE

We live in a world contaminated by sin. Sin is anything that goes against God's holy standards. When we do not follow the guidelines that God our Creator gave us, we are guilty of sin. Sin separates us from God, the source of life.

Since the time when the first man and woman, Adam and Eve, sinned in the Garden of Eden, sin has been universal. The Bible says that we all have "sinned and come short of the glory of God" (Romans 3:23). It also says that the natural consequence for that sin is eternal death, or punishment in an eternal hell: "Then when lust hath conceived, it bringeth forth sin: and sin, when it is finished, bringeth forth death" (James 1:15).

But we do not have to suffer eternal death in hell. God provided forgiveness for our sins through the death of His only Son, Jesus Christ. Because Jesus was perfect and without sin, He could die in our place. "For God so loved the world that he gave his only begotten Son, that whosoever believeth in him should not perish, but have everlasting life" (John 3:16).

A sacrifice is something given to benefit someone else. It costs the giver greatly. Jesus was God's sacrifice. Jesus' death takes away the penalty of sin for everyone who accepts this sacrifice and truly repents of their sins. To repent of sins means to be truly sorry for and turn away from the things we have done that have violated God's standards. (Acts 2:38; 3:19).

Jesus died, but He did not remain dead. After three days, God's Spirit miraculously raised Him to life again. God's Spirit does something similar in us. When we receive Jesus as our sacrifice and repent of our sins, our hearts are changed. We become spiritually alive! We develop new desires and attitudes (2 Corinthians 5:17). We begin to make choices that please God (1 John 3:9). If we do fail and commit sins, we can ask God for forgiveness. "If we confess our sins, he is faithful and just to forgive us our sins, and to cleanse us from all unrighteousness" (1 John 1:9).

Once our hearts have been changed, we want to continue growing spiritually. We will be happy to let Jesus be the Master of our lives and will want to become more like Him. To do this, we must meditate on God's Word and commune with God in prayer. We will testify to others of this change by being baptized and sharing the good news of God's victory over sin and death. Fellowship with a faithful group of believers will strengthen our walk with God (1 John 1:7).